ANIMAL WEAPONS

By the same author, published by MacGibbon & Kee

———

WILDLIFE PRESERVATION

PHILIP STREET

Animal Weapons

WITH LINE DRAWINGS BY
MEGAN DI GIROLAMO

MacGibbon & Kee   London

Granada Publishing Limited
First published in Great Britain 1971 by MacGibbon & Kee Ltd
3 Upper James Street London WIR 4BP

Copyright © 1971 by Philip Street

ISBN 0 261 63244 2
Printed in Great Britain by C. Tinling & Co Ltd
Prescot and London

CONTENTS

ILLUSTRATIONS

INTRODUCTION

ALL animal life depends for its survival upon its ability to obtain sufficient food and its efficiency in avoiding or successfully combating the attacks of its predatory enemies so that sufficient members of each generation survive long enough to breed and ensure the maintenance of the population from one generation to the next. Offence and defence are thus vitally important aspects of the survival of animal species and of the balance of nature. If the predators' weapons were not efficient enough, they would be starved to extinction; and if their victims' defences were inadequate, they would be killed to extinction.

There are a few obvious ways in which animals overcome their prey, and a few equally obvious methods by which animals avoid attack by their more powerful enemies, but a complete survey of the animal kingdom reveals an astonishing variety both of predatory and defensive devices. One universal fact about all of these methods of attack and defence is that none of them achieves perfection. The most efficiently designed weapon of attack will still only enable its possessors to account for a proportion of their chosen victims, and the most perfect method of defence will only result in the protection or escape of a proportion of the predators' prey.

To borrow from modern phraseology, a study of the weapons which animals use in attack and defence does not explain what makes them tick, but it can go a long way towards explaining how they are able to go on ticking.

ANIMAL WEAPONS

CHAPTER I

Horns, Teeth and Feet

OF all animal weapons, horns, teeth and feet are the structures most obviously developed for use in attack and defence – the 'brute force' weapons, although horns and antlers are used more often as threat displays and status symbols than as devices for inflicting actual damage.

Modern classification recognises sixteen orders of living placental mammals, but in only two of these are horns produced. Among the order Perissodactyla, which comprises the horses and their relatives the tapirs and rhinoceroses, only the latter bear horns, which as we shall see are quite different in origin and structure from those produced by members of the order Artiodactyla, the majority of whose members possess horns of one type or another.

The Artiodactyla are a very large group of mammals, comprising the pigs, hippopotamuses and camels, which are without horns, and the deer, giraffes, sheep, goats, antelopes and cattle in which they are a prominent and important feature. These latter in fact constitute four separate families, the Cervidae or deer, the Giraffidae, containing only the giraffe and the okapi, the Antilocapridae to which belongs only one living species, the North American prongbuck, and the Bovidae, a very large family, consisting of the sheep, goats, antelopes and cattle.

Modern zoologists believe that the most primitive type of artiodactyl horn is the deer antler, which also happens to be the most complicated in its development, and that all other artiodactyl horns represent evolutionary developments from it. Deer antlers are remarkable in that they are produced solely for combat between stags at the breeding or rutting season, and are not normally used as weapons against other animals either for defence or attack. When the rut is over they are shed and new antlers are grown the following year; they become ready for use just before the rut. Only in the reindeer are antlers produced by both sexes, the reason for this remaining a mystery.

The growth of new antlers is a remarkable process. All that remains after the old antlers of the previous year have been shed are two knobs of bone, which are part of the top of the skull. They are covered by the skin of the head. It is on these knobs, or pedicles as they are called, that the new antlers are formed. The first sign of the growth of new antlers is the formation of two velvety knobs on the pedicles. In some species these develop within a fortnight of the shedding of the old antlers. Their velvety appearance is due to the fact that the covering skin carries a thick pile of fine hairs. The skin itself is richly supplied with blood vessels. It is very sensitive, tender and warm to the touch. It has the remarkable property of being able to form large quantities of bone, the antlers being laid down within it as a solid bone core.

Once these knobs have appeared the growth of the antlers is rapid, and in about three months development is complete. Some idea of the rate of bone formation can be gained from the fact that a really big pair of red deer antlers may consist of seventy pounds or more of dense bone. As the antlers grow, so does the covering skin, and therefore when growth is completed the whole antler is still covered with velvet. Because the velvet is so sensitive stags are careful to avoid knocking their antlers against anything at this stage.

As soon as the antlers are fully grown a ring of bone is laid down around the base of each, just above the point where it joins the pedicle. This burr, as it is called, presses outwards and stretches the overlying velvet, gradually constricting the blood vessels passing out to the antler, and finally stopping the flow of blood altogether. Deprived of its blood supply the velvet soon dies and becomes dried up. It is of course no longer warm and sensitive. The stag now proceeds to rub its antlers against trees and other suitable objects until the dead velvet is stripped off. For the short time this is taking place the antlers present a very tattered appearance.

Whatever the physiological mechanism controlling antler development may be, it is obviously closely bound up with the mechanism controlling reproductive activity, because the rut always follows soon after the antlers are out of velvet. How soon after the rut the antlers are shed depends upon the species, and can show great variation even between individuals of the same species.

The mechanism of antler shedding is as interesting as that of their growth. The base of the antler, between the burr and the pedicle, is gradually eaten away from inside by special cells in the blood. When the process is completed the antlers, including the burrs, just drop off.

Well-developed antlers are produced by stags only when they are several years old. In their first years they grow progressively bigger and more complex antlers until finally a full head is produced. The increase in antler size and complexity depends upon living conditions. If adequate food is available a full head will be developed earlier than if the animal is undernourished.

The enormous wastage of bone through antler growth and shedding is a great strain on a stag's resources. In order to produce a full head it needs many pounds of calcium and phosphate with its food each year. Ultimately this must come from the soil through the grass or leaves which it eats. Serious calcium deficiency in the soil may affect antler growth. After the exceptionally wet winter of 1947 malformed antlers, due to calcium deficiency in the grass, occurred in the Woburn herds of Père David, red and fallow deer.

It is because of their great need for calcium that some deer herds chew antlers after they have been shed. One might assume that antler chewing would occur mainly where there was a calcium deficiency in the soil, but the evidence is not conclusive. At Whipsnade shed antlers cannot be chewed because they are collected for the sake of tidiness, but the paddocks are periodically dressed with lime. Although the Whipsnade subsoil is chalk, it is still possible for the soil to be calcium deficient if the calcium is leached out by rain. At Woburn part of the park is dressed with lime every year, yet chewing of shed antlers is quite common.

Some interesting experiments on calcium deficiency and antler chewing were conducted at Ardverekie in Scotland just before World War II. Antler chewing there had always been common, and an analysis of the soil showed it to be deficient in calcium. In 1937 and again in 1938 the stags' diet was supplemented during the period of antler growth by cubes containing calcium salts. At the subsequent shedding of the antlers no chewing was observed in either year. Calcium feeding was discontinued in 1939, and in the autumn antler chewing was resumed.

Despite all the nutritional effort which goes into producing them, deer antlers are of little use as weapons against predators. Even if they were, their effectiveness would be limited, because they are fully grown and without velvet for only a few months in the year, leaving the deer defenceless for most of the time. Presumably when they were first evolved they played a more positive role as defensive weapons, but today their role has become reduced to that of status symbols and threat displays at the rutting season.

At the onset of the rut each of the older stags assembles a sizeable harem of hinds. Some fighting does occur but this is seldom serious, and battles in which a stag is killed are exceptional. A preliminary skirmish is usually sufficient to convince one stag of the other's superiority, so that he retires before any serious fighting breaks out.

Thus it happens that at the beginning of the rutting season the strongest stags acquire a substantial harem, which by continual chivvying they manage to keep within a limited territory. The weaker stags patrol the areas around these territories, roaring frequent challenges but usually exercising sufficient discretion to refrain from following them up. Their turn will come towards the end of the rut, when the strong stags become tired. They can then take over any hinds which have not yet been served.

The Giraffidae, represented today only by the giraffes and the forest-dwelling okapi, have small and simple horns which like deer antlers have a covering of skin but are not shed and regrown each year. Once a giraffe has grown its horns it keeps them for life. There is usually only one pair in addition to a median horn in front of them, but there may be two pairs. They develop as isolated bones beneath the skin, later fusing with the bones of the skull. Giraffe horns are known as 'ossicones'.

Giraffes are docile creatures, but they can use their horns as weapons of attack, swinging their long necks round in order to bring their tiny horns into play with considerable force. Occasionally zoo giraffes have attacked their keepers by this method. The evidence of one such attack was preserved in the old Giraffe House in London Zoo. In 1865 a big bull giraffe aimed its head at a keeper who managed to dodge out of the way, and the giraffe's head struck a wooden pillar. The very considerable dent was covered with a glass plate and a notice was placed beneath it to record the incident. One of the most important pieces of evidence used on its discovery at the turn of the century for placing the okapi in the same family as the giraffe as its only living relative was its possession of ossicones.

The horns of all the Bovidae are built upon the same plan. There is a central bony core outside which grows a horny covering. Neither is shed, and both go on growing throughout the life of the animal. The possible link between the skin-covered antlers of the Cervidae and the Giraffidae and the horn-covered horns of the Bovidae is provided by the single living member of the family Antilocapridae, the American prongbuck *Antilocapra americana*. This has a horn which is two-branched, thus resembling a simple antler, but it has a very thin horny covering similar to the horn of a bovid. Unlike the bovid horn, however, the covering of the *Antilocapra* horn is shed and replaced annually, in the manner of deer antlers. Skin and horn are not in fact fundamentally different. Both are products of the outer layer of the body, and it is conceivable that during the course of evolution the hairy skin covering the deer antler or the giraffe horn could have been replaced by a covering of horn which, like the antler velvet, was shed each year. It would then be a short step to develop a somewhat thicker and stronger covering of horn which was no longer shed, thus giving rise to the typical horn of the bovid.

Unlike the other groups of the Artiodactyla the Bovidae certainly do use their horns as weapons, but only of defence. They are all herbivores, and agression is not required to capture grass and plants! But if they believe themselves threatened they will not hesitate to attack. The Bovidae certainly earned the respect of the old-time white hunters in Africa. To them the most dangerous of all animals was not the lion, or even the crafty leopard, but the Cape buffalo, with its horn bases meeting in the midline and forming a great mass of bony armour right across its forehead.

Artiodactyl horns all have one feature in common, a core of bone, which may be covered either with skin (deer and giraffes) or with horn (prongbuck and the Bovidae). But the horn of the rhino is a completely different structure. It is developed from a compact mass of horny fibres which are really hairs growing out from the skin of the snout. There is no intimate connection between the horn and the underlying bone of the skull. Of the five species of rhino three – the two African and the Sumatran – have two horns, while the great Indian and the Javan species have only one horn. They are probably not very often used by the rhinos in combat with other animals, but any animal misguided enough to attack one of these extremely powerful creatures will find that a rhino horn is indeed a formidable weapon.

Possession of efficient and formidable weapons is certainly a main factor in saving many kinds of animal from extermination. But in the case of the rhinos this very feature has brought them dangerously near to extinction. For some curious reason both in Africa and in Asia rhino horn is traditionally believed to be an aphrodisiac and commands a high price, so that it has always been, and still is, worth while for poachers to take all the necessary risks to kill rhinos in order to sell the horn. Often no other part of the body is used, being merely left to rot where it was shot or trapped. As old traditional weapons were replaced by more efficient modern firearms, so the threat to the rhinos grew. Considerable efforts have been made during this century to save all five species from extinction, and in this work no task has been greater or more important than curbing the activities of the poachers both in Asia and in Africa.

Teeth of one sort or another are present in a great variety of animals, but it would clearly be impossible here to deal with all kinds of dentition. A few outstanding examples will be chosen in which teeth play an unusual role. Mammals have three basic types of teeth: incisors, usually used for nibbling; canines, used for killing and tearing flesh; and molars (including premolars), used to grind or cut food. The extent to which each type is developed depends upon the mammal's particular method of dealing with its diet.

In a few species teeth are developed into exceptionally large tusks, the most remarkable of these being found in the walrus, the narwhal and the elephant. In the walrus the upper canines, gleaming white and dagger-like, point straight downwards. In the male they may be as much as three feet in length and weigh as much as twelve pounds each. In the female they are slimmer and usually not so long. Being of pure ivory they have a considerable market value when obtained in sufficient quantity. Curiously, these enormous tusks are not primarily used as weapons against other large animals. The walrus feeds on bivalve molluscs which live buried in the sand and mud on the sea bed, and its tusks are used to dig them up.

If necessary, though, walrus tusks can prove to be formidable weapons. Although they would never be rash enough to engage a full grown walrus, polar bears will sometimes attack an apparently isolated pup. Sometimes, however, they make a mistake, and the parents suddenly appear. Walruses have been known in such cases to chase the bear into the water and kill it with their tusks. In fact so well is it armed that the walrus's only effective enemy apart from man is the killer whale.

The most spectacular, and the most unusual of all tusks are those of the elephant. In all other mammals possessing tusks these are invariably over-developed canine teeth. The elephant develops no canine teeth and only two incisors, the two outermost in the upper jaw, and it is these which grow to form the tusks. They are composed almost entirely of solid ivory, and consequently are extremely heavy. They are also valuable, and constitute the poacher's most coveted prize. The elephant does not often have to use its tusks as weapons, but like the atom bomb they do constitute a formidable deterrent.

Among fish three types stand out on account of their teeth. Most fish have efficient teeth with which they are able to capture their prey but these three are feared by man wherever they occur. The best known of them are the sharks, many of which are able to remove great chunks of flesh, leaving jagged, bleeding tears. But the barracudas and the piranhas, although much smaller, are perhaps even more fearsome.

The barracuda, sometimes known as the tiger of the sea, is a smallish fish shaped rather like a pike and provided with a formidable array of long, pointed teeth. Barracudas occur in nearly all tropical waters. Native fishermen and divers have always had a greater fear of barra-cudas than they have of sharks. They will often dive in the company of sharks, but the approach of even a single barracuda is sufficient to send them rushing for safety. Barracudas are generally two to three feet in length, but the most fearsome member of the family, the giant barracuda of the West Indies, can grow to eight feet, and is capable of cutting clean through a man's arm or leg in one bite.

Man-eating sharks and barracudas are fearsome creatures, but for sheer ferocity and danger to man nothing that swims in the sea can match a small fish which lives in the rivers of South America. This is the piranha, which in spite of its proved reputation as a man-eater seldom exceeds seven inches in length, with ten inches almost a record.

Theodore Roosevelt, naturalist and President of the United States of America, first drew attention to this little fish in the early years of this century. He came back from an expedition to hitherto unexplored regions of South America with stories about the piranha which took some believing, but subsequent investigations have more than substantiated the claims he made on its behalf.

Death by sharks or barracudas is generally swift, and certainly merciful when compared with death as administered by piranhas. Any person or animal unfortunate enough to fall into a stretch of river infested by these bloodthirsty fish is literally eaten alive. Hundreds of them appear from nowhere, and the victim's flesh is removed in tens of thousands of tiny mouthfuls until nothing but the cleaned skeleton remains. Their gruesome work is short. In a recent investigation a 400 lb pig carcase was lowered into a river where piranhas were known to be abundant. Within ten minutes only the bones remained.

Although small, the piranha has an incredibly efficient set of sharp teeth, capable of making a clean bite right through a finger, bone included, at one go. Piranhas are normally quiet fish, but the arrival of a victim seems to work them into a frenzy, and it is not entirely hunger which drives them on. Long after they have eaten all they need they continue their savage attacks until no particle of flesh remains, the surplus mouthfuls piling up on the bottom of the river to be carried away by the current.

Nothing living escapes their attention, even their own kind, and it is impossible to keep more than one in an aquarium tank. There is a certain mystery about where they all come from when some person or animal falls into the water. Normally it seems that each individual has its own length of river, and there may be only two or three in a 100-yard stretch. This isolation is probably necessary for their own survival, because if they lived closer together they would soon kill one another. Yet in spite of this segregation hundreds can appear at one spot within minutes to deal with a victim; during these orgies they apparently take no notice of one another. As soon as the feat is over they presumably disperse, each making its way back to its own stretch of river. Of course the formidable teeth of sharks, barracudas and piranhas are not primarily designed as weapons against humans, but what we know of such attacks gives us a good idea of their effectiveness against their normal natural enemies.

Although vertebrates are the most prominent group to use teeth as weapons they are not unique in having developed teeth specifically for attack. The other major group in which teeth play a dominant part in the obtaining of food is the group of terrestrial and aquatic snails. Snails belong to the phylum Mollusca, of which there are two main divisions. The gastropod molluscs usually have a single shell which is nearly always coiled, giving them all a snail-like appearance, while the lamellibranch molluscs have a shell consisting of two halves or valves hinged along one common edge. Cockles, mussels and oysters are familiar members of this group.

Snails eat by means of a remarkable structure called the radula. This consists essentially of a long ribbon set with more than two thousand minute teeth arranged in several rows. Normally it is withdrawn within the mouth cavity, but whenever the creature feeds it is protruded through the mouth and scraped backwards and forwards, the tiny pieces of plant food rasped off in this way being passed back into the mouth to be swallowed. The radula grows continuously throughout the life of the animal, and as the teeth on the front part wear out the next section, containing new teeth, moves up to replace it.

Most marine snails are vegetarian, but there are a few important carnivorous species which feed upon other molluscs. The best known of these is the dog whelk, *Nucella lappillus*, a common species on seashore rocks. The radula of the dog whelk is much thinner than that of the vegetarian snails, with fewer but more prominent teeth, and can be protruded as a proboscis a considerable way out of the mouth.

With this proboscis the dog whelk, perched on a limpet, top shell, acorn barnacle or mussel, will bore a neat round hole in its shell. This is a laborious process and takes many hours, but when at last it is completed the proboscis can be thrust right through the hole. The flesh of the victim is then rasped away and carried back to the mouth in minute particles.

There are two other important British marine carnivorous snails: the sting winkle, *Ocenebra erinacea*, and the oyster drill, *Urosalpinx cinerea*. The sting winkle has a distinctive greyish brown shell with prominent ribs, which give it a very spiky appearance. Empty specimens washed in by the tide are often found among shingle. They have often lost much of their colour and appear greyish white. The sting winkle is one of the principal enemies of the oyster, and a great pest on the oyster beds, boring through the shells and devouring their contents with its long thin proboscis in the same way as the dog whelk destroys mussels. To the oyster fishermen the creature's proboscis is its sting, from which its name is derived.

The oyster drill was not originally a British species, but has become established here since the beginning of this century. In this period several unsuccessful attempts have been made to establish the American oyster on the English oyster beds to supplement the dwindling stocks of native oysters. Unfortunately in the process several of the serious pests of the American oyster beds were also brought over accidentally, among them the oyster drill, and although the oysters themselves failed to survive for any length of time, these pests have thrived and spread, transferring their attentions to our native oysters with serious consequences. Their method of dealing with their prey is precisely the same as that adopted by the sting winkles and dog whelks, shells being bored and the contents extracted by a long thin proboscis.

So hardy is the oyster drill that it can withstand cold weather better than our native dog whelks and sting winkles. In the exceptionally cold winter of 1928–9 the Essex oyster beds were practically cleared of these native species, but the oyster drills remained unaffected. During the next few years they multiplied rapidly, having to contend with little competition.

Feet play an important role as the principal weapons in many kinds of mammals and birds. All members of the horse family, including the zebra, are able to administer devastating kicks with both their front and hind feet. A mare with a foal has been known to put an attacking grizzly bear to flight with courageous and well-directed kicks. The principal weapon of the bear itself is its enormously muscular front feet with their immense paws, each armed with five long claws; one blow can split open a man's head. Usually the teeth are brought into use only to tear the victim's body to pieces.

The kick of the larger kangaroos is also notorious. Its feet are provided with strong blunt nails, and when cornered it sits up resting on its tail and aims a downward blow at its adversary with one or both hind legs. There is sufficient strength in such a kick to rip open the whole length of a man's body.

For perfection of design nothing can approach the feet of the members of the cat family, with their cruel curved and completely retractile claws which are as sharp as needles. As with bears, the prey is brought down with a blow from the front paws, after which the *coup de grâce* may be administered by a bite in the back of the neck. Again as with bears, the victim is then torn to pieces with the powerful teeth.

The large flightless birds, the ostrich, emu and cassowary, use their feet to kick their enemies in a similar manner to the kangaroo. The ostrich has only two very powerful toes terminating in a blunt nail on each foot. Cassowaries and emus have three toes on each foot, those of the emus being of similar size, whereas the inner toe on each foot of the cassowary has a long and exceptionally sharp nail. Any of these birds can cause serious injury with a well-directed kick.

But it is birds of prey which have evolved the most formidably aggressive feet. As with the cats and the bears, it is the feet of these birds which constitute their major weapon, not their beaks, which are

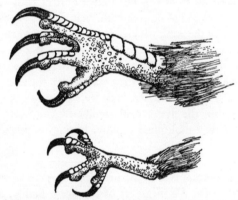

The powerful talons of the eagle (above) and the osprey are used for seizing their prey

used only to tear the captured prey to pieces. The general method of capture used is to fly at their victims when they are on the wing and grasp them with dagger-like talons. The osprey drops from the sky and plunges its legs into the water, where the talons sink into a fish swimming near the surface. An eagle's feet are said to be so powerful that it is impossible even for a strong man to loosen the grip of a single toe when the foot is grasping its prey, but few of us would wish to verify this statement. If an eagle is surprised on the ground without sufficient time to take to the air it will defend itself by lying on its back and brandishing its talons.

Gregarious animals which live in large herds have considerable potential for protecting themselves against their enemies if they could only realise the value of collective defence. Few species have developed a system of positive collective security, but one or two have discovered that by combining together they can often defeat attacks by animals individually much more powerfully armed than they are.

Herds of wild horses have long been known to defend themselves in this way from surprise attacks by packs of wolves. One of the first authentic accounts was given by the nineteenth-century authority Vogt in his *Natural History of Animals*.

> The herds live under the leadership of some old males, which have to watch over the well-being of their subjects. We cannot but admire the courage of these proud creatures, which, seeming to rejoice in battle, dart down upon an attacking carnivore, the whole herd arranging itself in a circle with the foals in the middle, and all ready to strike with the hoofs of their hind legs. In fighting with wolves, stallions try to seize their antagonists with their teeth by the nape of the neck, then to lift them up and dash them to the ground, after which they trample them underneath their feet. But these battles, from which perhaps the military art has derived the formation of squares, are only exceptions to the rule, and take place only in cases of sudden attack or when the herds are driven to straits. Usually the herd seeks its safety in rapid flight. Tearing along in furious gallop, with ears and mane erect, the herd dashes away with the speed of the wind, driving their young ones before them, the males galloping on the flanks and at the end of the column to protect the herd in its hurried flight.

Baboons have a highly developed sense of collective security. Mostly they live in considerable troops which may number several hundred individuals, and which are led by a number of old males. While the troop is feeding it is the duty of these leaders to maintain a careful watch for the approach of possibly dangerous enemies. Vogt is again worth quoting.

> On the approach of danger warning sounds are heard, and the females and the young then crowd together, while the old males, like the champions of the ancient Greeks, advance into the foremost of the fight uttering fearful cries, bellowing, and gnashing their teeth. A bold and proud spirit with contempt of death is beyond question a characteristic trait of the baboons, and when Brehm records a case in which an old Arabian male baboon gradually managed to extricate a young one, which had been left behind on a rock surrounded by

dogs, from the midst of its assailants and before the very eyes of the hunters, inspiring by its determined bearing both dogs and hunters with such respect for its powers that no attack was ventured on, we may well agree with Darwin in saying that here was proof of heroism of which only few men were capable.

At their drinking places on river banks the baboons' great anxiety is the appearance of crocodiles. In consequence they never drink without veteran guards being posted to watch out for these dreaded enemies. Vocal warnings at the first sign of danger send the whole troop rushing for safety, from which they will not emerge until the guards are satisfied that the danger is past.

Their extremely well-developed sense of collective security makes baboons among the most difficult of all animals to capture alive. The method usually adopted by professional hunters seeking specimens for zoos is to study a troop for some time until all its drinking pools have been discovered. All but one of these is then barred by fencing them round with cut thorn bushes.

To attract the baboons to the remaining pool all kinds of favourite foods are scattered around. After a few days, when the animals have regained their confidence, a basket-work cage made of saplings, with a long cord attached to its raised door, is placed in position and baited beside the pool. When the troop next approaches to drink, some of the baboons are lured into the cage and the door closes with a bang.

For a moment the captives sit petrified with terror, and then pandemonium breaks out. Unholy screams from within are answered with equally blood-curdling yells from without, as the rest of the troop attack the trap in an attempt to release their imprisoned comrades. For the hunters this is the crisis. In a short time the trap will be demolished. The would-be rescuers must thus be driven off at once. This can usually be achieved, but occasionally the hunters underestimate the strength of the troop.

Carl Hagenbeck, the great German zoologist and animal dealer, recalls one occasion when his hunters came near to losing their lives when they set a trap, perhaps rather recklessly, in the territory of a huge troop of baboons estimated to be 3,000 strong. No sooner had the door of the trap been closed on a number of captives than the rest of the troop attacked.

To the hunters it must have seemed like a nightmare as the savage hordes with bared teeth and erect manes, and uttering terrible screams, rushed upon them. Despite their firearms and cudgels their position was critical, but they managed to retreat. The attackers then turned their attention to the trap. With concentrated fury they flung themselves on it, reducing it to a complete wreck and departing with their released fellows.

Without doubt the animal with the most sophisticated system of collective security is the musk-ox, *Ovibos moschatus*. Zoologically it is one of a particularly interesting group of animals known as goat-antelopes, which is intermediate in structure between the two major groups of antelopes and goats. There are only a few species scattered about the world and living either in the far north or high up among mountain ranges. They are thus a group of extremely hardy species.

The musk-ox lives in the Arctic wastes of North America and Greenland, and in appearance it bears little resemblance either to a goat or to an antelope, being in general build like a small member of the ox family. A full-grown bull stands about five feet high at the shoulders and weighs between five and eight hundredweight. The wide, flattened bases of the horns meet across the front of the skull to form a complete shield, as they do in bison and buffalo. Although it is a fairly thick-set animal, with short sturdy legs, it appears to be more massive than it really is by virtue of its extremely thick coat. No animal is better adapted for life on the frozen Arctic wastes, and this coat is one of its important assets.

Musk-oxen are gregarious animals, commonly found in mixed herds of between twenty and thirty. On being attacked, usually by wolves, they never attempt to run away, but form up into a tight circle surrounding the calves. As the wolves close in they are received with lightning thrusts of the formidable horns, against which there is little chance of success. If the attackers persist for long, three or four adult bulls may suddenly break away from the herd and charge, causing the wolves to retreat in disorder.

Against human hunters this otherwise useful form of collective security proved a serious disadvantage. Packs of dogs were used to attack the oxen, keeping out of harm's way themselves and driving the oxen into their close defensive formation. It was then a simple matter for the hunters to shoot down the whole herd.

Speed as a weapon plays a significant part in the lives of many animals, enabling either an animal to escape from its pursuing enemies or a predator to overtake and capture fast-moving prey. Antelopes and horses are excellent examples of mammals which have become modified in structure to enable them to move with extreme rapidity over open ground,

The carnivores which prey upon them must also be gifted with a good turn of speed if they are to have any hope of catching them. Their usual technique is to lie in wait until a suitable victim comes within range so that they only have a short distance to run. All the large cats have remarkable acceleration and a high top speed, but they can make only relatively short dashes at maximum speed. If the pursued animal is not caught in the first few hundred yards it is likely to escape because it can maintain its top speed over much greater distances than its pursuer.

The champions of acceleration are the leopard and the cheetah. Victor Pohl, in a book about African wildlife, describes how he once watched a leopard creep stealthily towards a duiker, a small kind of antelope, and then make a sudden attack. 'So incredibly swift was his act,' he wrote, 'that fifteen yards must have been covered in about half a second; but the slight noise he inevitably made in doing so roused the duiker to instant action, for he leapt yards away from where he had been standing the minutest fraction of a second before.'

Robert Sutherland, another writer on African animals, also pays tribute to the leopard's speed:

> No animal can surpass the leopard in concentrated fury of attack when thoroughly aroused, and when in this state it behoves the hunter to exercise extreme caution. No one who has not experienced it can have any notion of the speed with which they charge. The uninitiated might fondly imagine that a chance of dodging might be possible, but such is not the case. A streak of light cannot give much start to a leopard's charge.

The champion athlete among the large cats is, however, the cheetah. It is reliably reported to be capable of achieving a speed of 45 miles an hour in two seconds from a standing start, and to go on to a maximum speed approaching 70 miles an hour. But this can be sustained for only a few hundred yards. By comparison an Olympic-class sprinter can reach a speed of about 16 miles an hour in two seconds, and a maximum speed of about 25 miles an hour.

To match the speeds of their predators some antelopes are certainly capable of outstripping almost all other mammals. Three species – the African springbok, the Mongolian gazelle and the North American prongbuck – are credited with a maximum of 60 miles an hour, this speed making the latter the fastest land animal in the whole continent of America.

Speed is also extremely important to birds of prey, which need to fly much faster than their victims since they almost invariably catch them on the wing. Speeds in excess of 300 miles an hour have been claimed for a few species, but these are not reliably authenticated. Perhaps the most reliable report concerns the peregrine falcon: more than 200 miles an hour, recorded on more than one occasion by the pilot of an aeroplane flying alongside or in pursuit. The golden eagle, too, is certainly known to be capable of flying at at least 120 miles an hour.

Many stories are told to emphasise the incredible speed of birds of prey when chasing their victims. One of these will suffice. A shot snipe was plummeting to the ground when a hawk appeared as from nowhere travelling at an incredible speed, and had no difficulty in scooping up the snipe long before it had reached the ground.

CHAPTER 2

Protection by Burrowing

LARGE numbers of animals escape the attentions of their enemies by hiding under stones or in crevices, or indeed in any suitable place where they cannot easily be detected. Generally their bodies do not have to be specially modified for this type of life. In this chapter, however, we shall examine the considerable number of animals which are adapted by structure and by behaviour to a burrowing existence in sand, mud or rock, or construct for themselves tubes into which they retire when danger threatens. We shall also meet a few unusual species which actually hide away for safety in the bodies of other animals.

Although a stretch of sand, shingle or mud left exposed by the receding tide on the seashore or in a river estuary may appear to be completely lifeless, beneath its surface it is in fact teeming with living creatures belonging to a number of different groups. Many groups produce the odd member successfully adapted to a life buried in sand or mud, but the dominant animals in these habitats are the bivalve molluscs, most of whose members are burrowers. Only the annelid worms can show a comparable range of species similarly adapted.

Perhaps the best known and certainly one of the most successful of these hidden bivalves is the common cockle, *Cardium edule*. Unlike the mussel and the oyster, which live on the surface of rocks and stones and are firmly fixed to them, the cockle and indeed all of the burrowing bivalves are mobile. The foot of the cockle is a well-developed muscular organ with which it can plough its way through the sand, horizontally or vertically, at considerable speed. Surfacing when the tide is in, or dug up when the tide is out, it can use its foot to carry it along in a series of little jumps. To achieve this leaping movement the foot is first bent in the middle while the tip is pressed down on to the sand. It is then straightened suddenly like a spring being released, and the animal is sent either rolling along the sand or upwards into the water or the air.

All bivalve molluscs have two respiratory siphons at one end of the body. A respiratory current of water enters through one, the inhalant siphon, and after passing over the gills out through the other, the exhalant siphon. The majority of bivalve molluscs are suspension feeders, which means that they feed on the minute organisms which live sus-

pended in sea water. These are filtrated out from the respiratory current
as it passes through the body.

For both respiratory and feeding purposes any bivalve mollusc must
take in a continuous current of water so long as it remains covered by
water. When the tide goes out its activities are suspended until the water

The cockle lies buried just beneath the surface of sand or mud, the
openings of its inhalant (right) and exhalant siphons projecting into the
water. When the tide goes out these are withdrawn beneath the surface

comes in again. The cockle's siphons extend some way beyond the edge
of the shell. The cockle lies in the sand in such a position that these
siphons lie more or less vertically, with their external openings on or
slightly above the surface of the sand. Both openings are fringed with a
ring of filaments.

To rely on microscopic life for its food might seem to be a rather
meagre way of making a living, but in fact sea water is teeming with
such life. The population density on a really good cockle-bed is well-

nigh incredible. As many as one and a half million cockles to the acre are known to exist on some beds extending for several hundred acres.

The cockles, of which there are no fewer than eight common British species, are just one of a whole group of suspension feeding bivalves found in sand and mud and leading essentially similar lives. These include cyprinas, venus shells, artemis shells, carpet shells, trough shells and gapers.

One bivalve mollusc which can burrow rapidly in sand in an emergency is the razor shell. The sides of each valve are straight and parallel, the ends being also almost straight and at right angles to them, the whole shape of the shell approximating to that of a long, narrow rectangle. The two valves gape widely at the hind end to allow passage for the siphons, and at the front end for the well-developed powerful foot. The larger species, *Ensis siliqua*, is about seven inches long and one inch wide, and *Ensis ensis* is somewhat smaller.

Razor shells are widely distributed on sandy shores near the low-water mark, lying vertically with their siphons directed upwards and their feet downwards. When covered by the tide they move up towards the surface so that the ends of their short siphons project slightly into the water. As the tide recedes they go deeper, remaining quiescent some little way below the surface until the water returns.

Most other sand- or mud-burrowing bivalves can be dug out easily with a spade, but not so the razor shells. The slightest vibration causes them to sink at an amazing speed and the only hope of obtaining a specimen is to approach with extreme caution to avoid vibrating the sand, and then to plunge the spade right in and throw out the sand all in one movement. Even so, more razor shells will be missed or cut in half than are dug out whole. The position of a razor shell beneath the surface is often betrayed by a slight depression in the sand.

The slender shape of the shell and its extreme smoothness both help it to move swiftly, but the most important factor is the efficiency of its foot. This is very large, and when retracted it occupies at least half the space enclosed between the two valves. When the razor shell wants to go deeper it protrudes its foot vertically downwards. Since it is pointed it slides easily through the wet sand. When it is fully extended blood is pumped into the tip, which swells to a mushroom shape to form a firm anchor. The rest of the foot is then contracted, the whole shell thus being drawn down towards the swollen tip, which is then allowed to contract to normal proportions as the blood flows back into the body. To move upwards the foot is extended only a short way before the tip becomes swollen. As extension continues the shell is pushed upwards.

Both upward and downward movements can be repeated several times to cover greater distances than can be achieved by one extension or contraction of the foot.

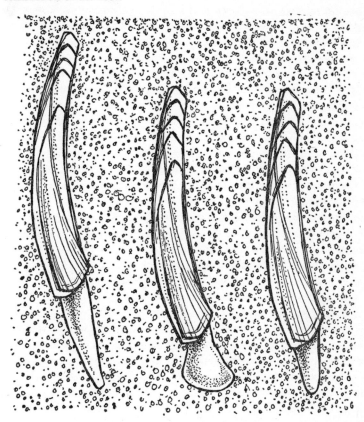

The razor shell uses its muscular foot to sink rapidly down through the sand

If a razor shell is thrown on to the surface of the sand it will immediately protrude its foot, turn it downward into the sand and anchor it. The subsequent pull up-ends the shell into a vertical position and drags it a little way down. A few repetitions will ensure that the shell disappears from view.

Not all the sand- and mud-burrowing bivalves are suspension feeders. Several groups have perfected a different method of feeding. On the surface of sand and mud there is always a layer of organic material settling from the water, and it is this which the deposit feeders gather. To enable them to obtain this material while lying buried beneath the surface they have long, thin flexible inhalant siphons which can be extended six inches or more beyond the hind end of the shell. These siphons are moved over the surface of the sand or mud with the opening facing downwards, the deposited organic material being sucked in with the inhalant water current just as the nozzle of a vacuum cleaner picks up particles of deposited dirt along with a current or air. The exhalant siphon is separate from the inhalant siphon in order to allow the latter maximum freedom of movement, and it is usually shorter because it does not have to extend beyond the surface of the sea bed. The best known deposit feeders are the various species of wedge shells, tellins, sunset shells and furrow shells. Most are brightly coloured, highly polished and flatter than most suspension feeders.

In nature there is of course no such state as complete safety, and while burrowing in sand or mud certainly puts them beyond the reach of many potential enemies, there are others whose own special adaptations enable them to prey upon these hidden bivalves. The activities of dog whelks, sting winkles and oyster drills on oyster and mussel beds have already been described in the first chapter. Two species of carnivorous snails, *Natica catena* and *Natica paliana*, have become as completely adapted to life beneath sand or mud as the burrowing bivalves, and they rely upon these bivalves for their food.

To enable them to plough their way through the sand their foot is much enlarged and very powerful. They work their way through the upper layers of the sand in search of the bivalves, and when a victim is found its shell is drilled and its body rasped out at leisure. In their drilling operations these snails are aided by a gland on the under surface of the proboscis with produces acid to dissolve the material of the shell.

Starfish, as we shall see in Chapter 5, are among the most effective enemies of mussels, oysters and other bivalve molluscs which live on the sea bed or on rocks above it. One species, however, differs in its habits from all the rest. Instead of gliding about on the sea bed or in rock pools, the burrowing starfish, *Astropecten irregularis*, lives buried in sand a little way beneath the surface. As it moves through the sand it finds an abundance of bivalve molluscs on which it can feed.

Like the starfish, the crabs too have their single representative specially adapted to a burrowing existence. The burrowing crab, *Corystes cassivelaunus*, has an oval carapace or shell on which there are furrows suggesting the outlines of a face. It is for this reason that the creature is also known as the masked crab. If a living specimen is placed on the surface of the sand it does not attempt to walk away but proceeds to sit up in a vertical position and dig down into the sand with forward and upward sweeping movements of the walking limbs. Within a very short time it has sunk out of sight, leaving only the tips of its very long antennae projecting above the surface to betray its presence.

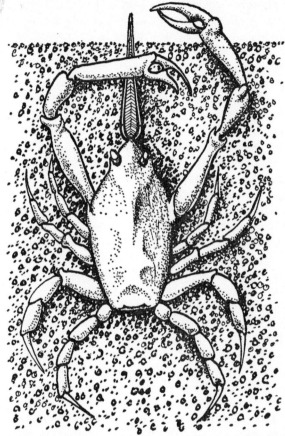

The burrowing or masked crab lies vertically in the sand, its specially modified antennae reaching up into the water

These antennae represent the masked crab's most important adaptation, enabling it to live in the sand. Normally a crab draws in a respiratory current of water at the sides of the thorax, passes it over its gills, and then gets rid of it through the front openings of the gill chambers, which lie on either side of the mouth. If the current flowed in the reverse direction particles of the crab's food might well be drawn in with it, and would thus foul the gills. When the masked crab lies buried, however, it would be impossible for it to maintain this current without

B

drawing in quantities of sand which would clog the gill chambers.

Close examination of the masked crab's antennae shows that each is provided with a double row of hairs, and that the two antennae interlock so that the four rows of hairs form a tube. When the crab lies buried in the sand the tip of this tube projects just above the surface clear of the sand, and down it a current of clean water is drawn. This enters the front openings of the gill chambers and leaves at the sides, thus reversing the normal direction of the respiratory current. This does not matter, because so long as the crab lies buried it does not feed. The hairs on the antennae are set sufficiently close together to prevent sand grains blocking the tube.

Corystes is thought to lie buried during the daytime to avoid the fish which would otherwise eat it. At night, however, it comes out of hiding to forage for food, and it is interesting that as soon as it surfaces it reverses the direction of its respiratory current, which now enters at the side of the carapace and leaves by travelling up the antennal tube.

The annelid worms, as already mentioned, are second only in abundance among the animals living in sand and mud. The large dark brown or black lug-worm, *Arenicola marina*, which fishermen dig up for bait, is one of the largest and most abundant of these burrowing worms. It is also one of the best examples of successful adaptation in structure and habits to a sedentary life completely buried in sand. It is a fat but rather flabby worm, often exceeding a foot in length, and with a body divided into three distinct parts, the middle portion bearing thirteen pairs of bright red gill tufts.

Although lug-worms will be found only by digging, there is evidence of their presence when the tide goes out in the familiar worm casts which are often so abundant on the shore. Like the earthworm, which swallows earth and digests what organic material it contains before passing it out as a worm-cast, the lug-worm swallows sand and passes it out as a cast on the surface after extracting such nourishment as it might contain. It is in fact the only shore worm to adopt this method of feeding. Lug-worms are less common in clean sand than in muddy sand, which contains a higher proportion of the decaying organic material providing them with their food.

Down in the sand the lug-worm inhabits a U-shaped burrow it has constructed. The cast covers the tail end of the burrow. Near it you will often be able to detect a shallow depression which indicates the position of the head end. The burrow is much longer than the worm, which normally lies in the horizontal gallery at the bottom, with its head at the base of the vertical shaft. This is about three times as wide as the tail shaft, and is kept filled with loose sand which the worm eats away from the bottom. The sand higher up the shaft slips down to replace it, resulting in the formation of the depression at the top when the tide is out. As the tide comes in again the depression is filled up, providing fresh supplies of sand for the worm to eat. Periodically the worm travels backwards to thrust its tail up the tail shaft to deposit a worm cast of digested sand at the surface. The tail shaft is kept free of sand.

Faced with the necessity of maintaining a continuous respiratory current of water over its gills the lug-worm has developed an ingenious method. By passing waves of contraction along its body from tail to head it draws a continuous stream of water down the tail shaft and up through the column of loose sand filling the head shaft. Periodically this sand tends to become clogged, and so restricts the flow of water through it. To loosen the sand the worm uses its head as a piston, repeatedly pushing it into the sand in the shaft and withdrawing it until the water will once more flow freely through it.

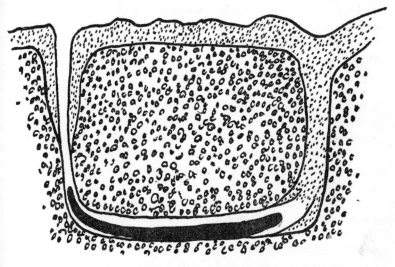

The lug-worm lying in its burrow, the tail shaft on the left being kept clear of sand

The lug-worm's burrow is merely dug in the sand, but many of the other species of burrowing worms construct permanent tubes in the sand or mud in which they live. These are amazing structures, each species having its own style of craftsmanship and using its own type of materials, which are cemented together with mucus. Some choose sand grains and others mud particles, according to the nature of the beach in which they live, while others construct their tubes out of a kind of parchment which they produce from their own bodies.

The sand mason, *Lanice conchilega*, is a common tube worm found on the lower parts of sheltered sandy beaches. Its tube is rough in appearance and is made from coarse sand grains. It usually projects a little above the surface of the surrounding sand. The tube itself is much longer than the worm, which retreats into the lower portion when disturbed and when the tide goes out. Pairs of special glands along the underside of the body produce the mucus used in tube building.

Like all the tube worms its structure is much modified to adapt it for its specialised life. At the head end it is provided with numerous thread-like outgrowths, which when the tide is in are thrust out through the mouth of the tube into the water. Some of these are gills collecting oxygen, and the others are tentacles with which the worm gathers its food, consisting of tiny particles of organic material which settle on the sand round about. The sand mason is thus a deposit feeder like some of the burrowing bivalve molluscs mentioned earlier. Tufts of bristles on the front segments and tiny hooks on all the segments enable the worm to grip the sides of the tube and withdraw itself quickly when danger threatens.

Tube worms look very attractive with their brightly coloured gills and tentacles waving gently about in the water. The most beautiful of them all are the fan or peacock worms, which have circles of very long tentacles. Their tubes are made of mud, and they live on sheltered muddy shores and in river estuaries. Unlike the sand mason they are suspension feeders, collecting minute organisms and organic particles suspended in the water, their tentacles being provided with cilia for this purpose.

When stones are turned on a shore where plentiful organic material darkens the sand, groups of thin red or orange threads may be revealed twisting about slowly on the surface. These are the gills and feeding tentacles of a burrowing worm known as red threads, *Cirratulus cirratus*. Although related to the tube builders it does not itself build a tube, being content merely to sink its body into the wet sand. It is not easy to dig this worm out of the sand intact, as it has a habit of shedding its tentacles and gills when disturbed.

Many stones and rocks carry what at first sight appear to be whitish and often wavy strips of limestone, each between one and two inches long, with a sharp ridge running along the top and ending in a sharp spine at the wider end. These are the calcareous tubes constructed for its defence by a small worm called *Pomatoceros triqueter*. If you put a stone carrying some of these tubes into water you may see the front end of the worm emerge, its tiny tentacles waving. These tentacles are ciliated, and are used like those of the fan worms for respiration and for suspension feeding. One of them has become modified as a club-shaped operculum, which is used to close the entrance to the tube when the worm withdraws inside it. Like all tube worms, they are sensitive to shadows and if, as you watch them, your shadow falls on them, they will withdraw into their tubes in an instant.

Convergent evolution, by which two completely unrelated types of animals evolve similar structures for a similar purpose quite independently of each other, is an extremely interesting phenomenon. There is certainly no possible connection between the various types of tube worms and the larvae of the caddis fly, yet these larvae, usually referred to as caddis worms, construct tubes for their protection which are remarkably similar to those produced by the marine annelids.

Adult caddis flies are not unlike small and rather sombre moths in general appearance, and like the majority of moths they are nocturnal in their habits. They are widely used by fly fishermen, to whom they are known as sedge flies.

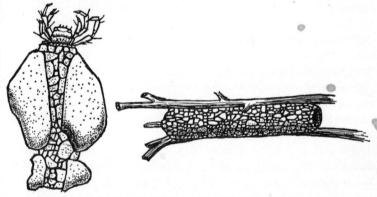

Caddis cases constructed by caddis fly larvae for their protection

Most caddis larvae are completely aquatic, and many of them build the familiar caddis cases in which they live. These consist of a lining of silk to which various materials may be attached. Each species usually has its favourite material for covering and strengthening its case, which usually therefore gives a strong clue to the identity of the species occupying it. Between them, however, they use almost anything occurring in the water, including pieces of leaves, stalks, sticks, sand, gravel and even the minute shells of very young water snails. The silk is produced by special glands which open into a spinneret on the floor of the mouth.

Caddis cases are tubular and open at both ends, the front opening being larger to allow the head and thorax to protrude when the creature moves along the river bed. When danger threatens they are rapidly withdrawn within the case. The head and the upper surface of the thorax are hard, and the three pairs of thoracic limbs are well developed for walking. All along the abdomen there are pairs of whitish thread-like gills, over which a constant respiratory current of water is drawn by undulatory movements of the abdomen. At the hind end there are two claspers which grip the case and ensure that it is pulled along as the creature moves. So firmly is the larva attached to its case by these claspers that it cannot be forcibly removed without severely damaging its body.

After about a year, when the larva has become full grown, it prepares to pupate. Most species fix their cases to a stone and cover both openings with a network of silk, which prevents the entry of enemies while at the same time allowing free access to the respiratory current of water. Pupation generally takes several weeks to complete, and in some species the adult does not emerge until the following spring, the pupal stage persisting through the winter. Caddis pupae have a pair of powerful mandibles with which they bite their way out of the case when it is time for the adult fly to emerge.

Some animals have so perfected the art of burrowing that they can excavate well-nigh impregnable, permanent tunnels in wood or rock. Economically they are extremely significant because of the immense damage they do to pier and jetty piles, harbour stonework and wooden ships.

The chief offender, and at the same time the most perfectly adapted of these borers, is the ship-worm, *Teredo navalis*. Since man first began to sail the seas in wooden ships the ship-worm must have been a major problem. Certainly we know that its ravages caused grave concern to Greek and Roman sailors.

The ship-worm is an excellent example of an animal which has become so modified to fit it for an unusual mode of life that its adult structure gives little obvious evidence of its family relationships. In spite of its worm-like appearance and its name, it is in fact a bivalve mollusc related to the many burrowing bivalves which have already been described.

The adult lives only in wood which is immersed in sea water, its specialisation making it impossible for it to live anywhere else. Each individual occupies a burrow about one quarter of an inch wide and up to a foot in length. These burrows are difficult to detect, because just before reaching the surface they narrow to a mere pinhole opening. The planks of a ship or the wooden piles of a pier can thus become honey-combed with ship-worm burrows without the fact being detected until they suddenly crumble. In earlier times many a ship must have foundered in mid-ocean through unsuspected infestation by the ship-worm.

At the inner end of the burrow is the front end of the animal, with its two tiny and much-modified shell valves with which the burrow is excavated. Each carries on its outer surface numerous rows of minute, sharp teeth, making it a very efficient rasp or file.

The adductor muscles, which in the normal bivalve mollusc serve to close up the valves, are modified in the ship-worm in such a way that their contraction rocks the two valves in turn. Instead of contracting simultaneously, the contractions alternate. Meantime the foot, by gripping the sides of the burrow, causes these rocking valves to be pressed against the end of the burrow to scrape away the wood. To ensure even excavation, the position of the valves is frequently changed by shifting the attachment of the foot. It is said that the scraping can be heard by placing the ear against a piece of infested wood. In the words of a seventeenth-century writer: 'They gnaw with their teeth and pierce into Okes, as you may know by the noise.'

The other end of the long body is fixed to the burrow just inside the tiny opening, through which two tubes can be protruded or withdrawn at will. These are the inhalant and exhalant siphons, characteristic of all bivalves. A respiratory current of water is drawn in through the one and passed out through the other after flowing over the gills and past the mouth. The long tube which connects the two ends of the body is really an elongated gill chamber, the gills forming the septum separating the inhalant and exhalant currents.

As the inhalant current passes the mouth, the cilia surrounding it remove minute plankton organisms and other tiny particles for food. Thus the ship-worm is a suspension feeder, though this accounts for only part of its diet. It is also able to digest the wood particles removed during its boring activities.

When disturbed or alarmed, it withdraws its siphons and closes the entrance to its burrow with the two small pieces of shell called pallets which are fixed to the body at the base of the tubes. Similar shelly material is used to line the burrow. The surface of badly infested timber sometimes becomes worn away, leaving the first inch or two of these shelly linings exposed.

Of course the ship-worm is an absolute prisoner within its burrow, and at the breeding season the reproductive products are merely passed out into the sea via the exhalant current. Here the eggs are fertilised and develop into minute larvae which soon form a pair of tiny bivalve shells and a foot. Any larva which manages to settle on a piece of wood rocks its tiny valves against the wood, and in a short time will have burrowed beneath the surface, leaving only the pinhole opening. Within the pinhole the ship-worm grows rapidly, and in a few months will have grown to full size and excavated its burrow.

Floating timber washed up on the shore is sometimes found to contain burrows made by another kind of wood-boring bivalve called *Xylophaga dorsalis*. This has two shell valves similar to those of the ship-worm, and it bores its way into the wood in the same way. Unlike the ship-worm, however, *Xylophaga* is incapable of digesting and extracting nourishment from the wood particles rasped off by the shell. It bores

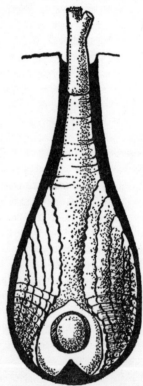

The piddock is able to excavate a protective burrow in rock, its siphons projecting into the water so long as the tide is in

only for protection. The burrows, too, are shallow, so that the animal remains just beneath the surface of the wood, and there is no long worm-like tube connecting the siphons with the remainder of the body within the shell valves. Ship-worms are capable of existing in wood only because they rely upon the wood for their nourishment, but specimens of *Xylophaga* sometimes excavate their homes in the insulating layers of submarine cables.

The best known of the rock borers are the various species of piddocks. The piddock is one of a group of bivalve molluscs known as gapers, in which the two shell valves remain apart to leave a gap at both the front and hind ends. Through the front gap the foot, modified as a sucker, can be protruded to grip the inner end of the tunnel, while through the gap at the opposite end the siphon tubes are extended. At their front ends the valves carry rows of minute teeth with which the rock is worn away as the burrow is excavated or enlarged. To do this the piddock takes a firm grip with its foot and then rocks and twists the whole shell by alternate contraction of the anterior and posterior adductor muscles, both of which are well developed. The two halves of the shell are not bound together by a hinge ligament as they are in most other bivalves, and this allows independent movement of the two valves. All the time the valves are pressed firmly against the rock.

When it first bores its way into the rock the piddock is quite a small specimen, so the opening of the burrow is usually small. Inside, however, the burrow opens out, because as the piddock grows it widens as well as lengthens its burrow. Sometimes piddocks burrow quite deeply into the rock, and to compensate for this their siphons are capable of considerable extension to enable them still to reach the mouth of the burrow to draw in the respiratory water current.

The piddocks' boring mechanism must be very efficient, because they are found in almost any but the hardest rocks, though they do tend to be rather more common in the softer sandstones, shales and chalk. Despite the hard work which they have to do, the shell valves are quite thin but nevertheless strong. One curious fact about piddocks is that although they spend virtually the whole of their lives hidden away in rocks they are among the most strongly phosphorescent of all marine animals. Seen in the dark the whole surface of the body is suffused with a powerful greenish-blue light.

Mention has already been made of the accidental introduction into Britain of the American oyster drill during abortive attempts to establish the American oyster on our beds. At the same time an American rock borer, *Petricola pholadiformis*, was also accidentally introduced here. Although similar in its habits to the piddocks it is not closely related to them.

The largest species of piddock is the common piddock, *Pholas dactylus*, a full-grown specimen of which may measure as much as six inches in length. There are two much smaller rock borers, *Hiatella gallicana* and *Hiatella arctica*, which seldom exceed one and a half inches in length. The front ends of the valves are not toothed but wrinkled, and they are usually found only in soft rock. The ends of their siphons, which can be seen at the entrance to the burrows, are red, and for this reason these two species are often known locally as 'red noses'.

Although in earlier times it was sometimes suggested that these various rock-boring molluscs were aided chemically in their operations by the production of acids which would help by dissolving the rock, all the species so far considered do in fact rely entirely upon mechanical means to excavate their burrows. There is, however, one kind of bivalve which does make use of chemical action in burrowing. It is the date mussel, *Lithophagus lithophagus*, a Mediterranean species which in size, shape and colour resembles a ripe date.

A special gland produces acid which dissolves limestone and chalk, and this limits the distribution of the date mussel to these rocks, since the acid would have no effect on non-calcareous rocks. Special provision has to be made to protect the date mussel's own calcareous shell from the effects of the acid it produces, and this is achieved by providing it with a complete additional outer layer of horny material which is impervious to acid. The shell itself, not having to stand up to mechanical boring, does not need to be so tough as the shells of other rock borers, and is in fact quite thin and delicate. In closely related bivalves which do not burrow the acid gland is absent.

In parts of the Mediterranean region ancient borings made by date mussels thousands of years ago provide unusual evidence of the rise and fall of land over a period of several thousand years. The best-known example is at Pozzuoli, near Naples. Here the limestone pillars of the Temple of Seraphis are still standing, and for several feet up they are riddled with date mussel burrows. Certainly when the temple was built it was on dry land, as it is today. But during the intervening years the land must at some time have sunk sufficiently for it to have been covered by the sea to a depth of several feet. Only then could the date mussels have carried out their excavations. Later still the land must have risen again to bring the temple once more above sea level.

Bivalve molluscs are not the only animals capable of boring into wood.

A tiny crustacean wood borer called the gribble probably causes more damage than any other boring animals except ship-worms. Pier piles and breakwaters are often seen apparently rotting away towards the bottom. In many cases the gribble will be the cause. It was discovered about 180 years ago by a famous lighthouse builder, Robert Stevenson, destroying the timbers of the Bell Rock lighthouse off the Firth of Forth. This tiny creature, related to the woodlouse, has a length of only about one fifth of an inch. With its pair of powerful jaws it eats away the wood to make a burrow, and its seven pairs of short legs end in sharp claws with which it retains its hold on the wood.

Unlike the ship-worm, it is only the adult gribbles which begin burrowing. Having constructed a burrow, they can leave it and swim about in the sea, later making a new burrow elsewhere if they want to. These burrows do not run far into the wood. They are usually about two inches long and run obliquely in from the surface. At intervals tiny 'manholes' connect the burrow with the surface, making it easier for a respiratory current of water to be maintained into and out of it.

Each burrow is usually occupied by a pair of gribbles, and since the female always seems to be in front of the male at the inner end it appears that she must be responsible for most of the excavating work. There is an interesting difference in the behaviour of the two sexes when they are disturbed. The male backs out of the burrow, but the female clings to the wood and braces herself against the sides so effectively that only by doing her serious injury can she be dislodged.

One species of sponge, known as the boring sponge, has the ability to bore holes in limestone rock, living just beneath the surface in a honeycomb of passages. It is believed to dissolve away the rock with acid. The boring sponge also lives on certain mollusc shells, to which it does serious damage by its boring activities. It sometimes becomes a serious pest on the oyster beds, so eating away the shells that they crumble to the touch, which makes the oysters commercially valueless. On some Continental beds, the oysters are grown on wooden frames which are periodically taken out of the water during rainy weather. The oysters close up tightly and are unharmed, while the fresh water soon kills the sponges.

Perhaps the most unusual of all the methods adopted by animals to hide from their potential enemies is to take up residence within the shells and sometimes even the bodies of other animals. One of the best known of these fugitives is the pea crab, *Pinnotheres pisum*, an inhabitant of British seashores. Males grow to a maximum width of one quarter of an inch, the females growing somewhat larger. For protection they take up residence within the shells of mussels, obtaining the food they require by extracting it from the suspended food trapped by the mussels, and perhaps supplementing this by taking occasional nibbles at their hosts' gills.

Full-grown female pea crabs sometimes grow too large to be able to leave the mollusc shell, where they are thus confined for the remainder of their lives. This is no hardship to them except at the breeding season, for there is always a plentiful supply of food for them to raid. The breeding difficulty is overcome by mating visits of the smaller male to the imprisoned female. The fertilised eggs are shed into the mantle cavity of the mussel, whence they are carried to the exterior in the outgoing respiratory current. It is an interesting fact that pea crabs are generally found only in well-nourished mussels.

The female of another tiny crab also finds itself a prisoner in its living home when it reaches full size. This is the gall crab, *Hapalocarinus*, found only in tropical seas, where it lives within coral. Coral consists of huge colonies of animals looking much like tiny sea anemones, to which they are in fact closely related. Unlike anemones, however, each individual coral animal builds a hard calcareous cup around its base. Because the members of the colonies live close together these cups join up to form great masses of limestone. Each generation of coral animals forms its cups on top of those left by earlier generations, and in this way massive coral reefs are built up.

The young female gall crab chooses for its future home a small space surrounded by young coral animals. As they grow they adjust the shape of their cups so as to form a cavity in which the crab can live in complete safety, making it large enough for the crab when it has eventually grown to full size. A small opening is left through which the imprisoned female crab can draw in a current of water for feeding and respiration. The males live outside the coral, and as they are much smaller than the females they can pass through the openings into the cavities to visit them at the breeding season.

Perhaps the most remarkable of the animals which live for protection within the bodies of other animals are the pearlfish, found in tropical seas in many parts of the world. They have chosen for their hideout the anus of the sea cucumber, a curious relative of the starfish and sea urchins. Some of them apparently live out their entire lives in the hind gut of their adopted hosts, while others come out at night when danger threatens least to feed on shrimps and other small crustaceans. In some populations of sea cucumbers as many as half of the individuals are found to have these extremely slender fish living in the hindgut.

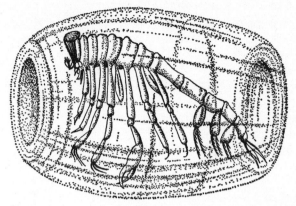

The small planktonic crustacean *Phronima* lives for protection within the
empty tunic of a salp which it has attacked and eaten

Enormous numbers of small crustaceans live in the surface layers of
the sea, where they form a considerable proportion of the animal
plankton. Krill, for example, form the principal food of the blue, fin and
humpback whales, and *Calanus* provides the herrings with the major
part of their diet. One of these small planktonic crustaceans, *Phronima*,
has evolved a novel method of protecting itself from the hazards of
planktonic life. In the plankton there are large numbers of small
creatures called salps, which live within a transparent barrel-shaped
gelatinous shell or tunic, open at both ends, which they themselves have
produced. *Phronima* attacks such a salp, eats the contained animal and
thus takes over its barrel-shaped tunic as its home. In this comandeered
home it can feed and produce its young. In samples of living plankton a
female *Phronima* has been seen pushing in front of it a barrel full of
young.

CHAPTER 3

Shells for Defence

MANY different kinds of animals construct external skeletons of various kinds, popularly known as shells, within which their soft bodies are given some protection from their potential enemies. Among these some of the most successful are the crabs and lobsters, the larger kinds of which are able to lay down shells of considerable thickness and strength.

Crabs and lobsters are crustaceans, which in turn are members of the phylum Arthropoda including also the insects, spiders, scorpions and the mites and ticks. All arthropods have a segmented body enclosed in an external skeleton consisting fundamentally of chitin. Chitin is a horny, flexible material, but over much of the body it is often strengthened with a variety of other substances which also make it rigid. Between consecutive segments, except in the head region, the chitin usually remains unstrengthened, as it does also between the joints of the limbs, thus giving flexibility both to the trunk and to the limbs.

In the crabs and lobsters the skeleton is strengthened by extensive calcification, calcium carbonate being deposited within the layer of chitin, giving it considerable strength and rigidity. In the head region the chitin between the segments as well as that on the segments is strengthened in this way, so that the whole head is covered with a rigid skeleton. The skeletons of a varying number of thoracic segments are similarly strengthened and fused together to give added protection. Further protection is given by a fold of calcified chitin which begins at the back of the head and continues over some of the trunk segments as a protective shield for the back. It also bends downwards so as to cover the sides, and may in addition become fused with the dorsal parts of the thoracic skeleton. This fold is called the carapace, and together with the head skeleton it forms the hard shell of the crabs and lobsters.

While an external skeleton has many advantages it also has one great disadvantage. Once it has been laid down it becomes impossible for the animal within to grow in size. It must therefore be shed periodically and replaced by one slightly larger. This moulting, or ecdysis, is brought about by enzymes which dissolve the inner layers of chitin, enabling the occupant to split and slide out of the old skeleton. While the body is increasing in size and a new larger skeleton is being formed crabs and lobsters go into hiding, because without the protection of a skeleton they are extremely vulnerable to all kinds of enemies. Before ecdysis is due to begin the crustacean lays down a considerable store of food within its body. The body is increased in size through a rapid intake of fluid during the short time necessary for the new skeleton to be laid down and hardened.

If a crab is picked up by one of its legs or claws it may give a sudden jerk and run off leaving a severed limb in your hand. This need cause no alarm, for it is a defence mechanism. One of the dangers which all creatures living on the sea bed have to face is the possibility of getting their limbs caught beneath stones rolled about by the moving water. As a method of escape crabs shed trapped limbs with little lasting inconvenience to themselves, a phenomenon known as autotomy. These breaks always occur at the third joint of the limb, counting from the body. At this joint there is a special autotomiser muscle, contraction of which serves to break the limb along a special breaking plane. No muscles are severed, and the broken ends of the nerves and blood vessels are very quickly sealed by a clot of blood.

At the next moult a miniature new limb makes its appearance, and this grows bigger with each succeeding moult, until eventually the replacement limb becomes as large as and indistinguishable from its undamaged fellow on the other side of the body. This ability to regenerate lost limbs was the basis of a cruel practice which prevailed among Spanish fisherman at a time when crab claws had a high market value. They would remove the claws from any crabs they caught and then throw the crabs back into the sea so that they might each eventually provide another pair of claws.

Adult crabs probably moult once a year, but more frequently if conditions are particularly favourable, and it is an extremely neat process. A split appears in the shell immediately behind the carapace, and the naked crab emerges backwards through this crack. The discarded shell is wonderfully complete and really looks like a whole crab, with the outer covering of the eyes and the horny layer and teeth which line the crab's stomach. Young crabs grow more quickly than adults, and for the first year or two at least they moult several times a year.

Moulting serves another useful purpose besides enabling the crab to grow. The back of a crab's carapace offers a particularly suitable site for barnacles and other sedentary organisms, and crab shells often become encrusted with them. The crab is unable to dislodge these uninvited guests through its own efforts but when the old shell is moulted they are discarded along with it.

To be unable to move, living as a fixture to a seashore rock, to have to rely for food upon such microscopic particles as the returning tide may bring within reach, and lacking means of capturing larger prey, hardly suggests a flourishing mode of life. Yet the little acorn barnacles which endure this apparently limited existence are among the most successful of all shore animals. It has been estimated that there may be more than 1,000 million of them along a mile stretch of rocky shore.

Acorn barnacles are among the most obvious of all seashore animals, occurring on almost every rock face which is not covered with weed, and often on stones and shells as well. First-year specimens are most numerous, each looking like a tiny flattened whitish cone of shell about one eighth of an inch across. Often there are so many that little of the actual rock can be seen between them.

For a long time these acorn shells puzzled naturalists, who classed them as molluscs because they looked like tiny limpets. A study of their development from the egg, however, showed that they belonged to the Crustacea, and were thus related to the crabs, shrimps, prawns and lobsters. The microscopic larvae which hatch out from the barnacle eggs are typical crustacean larvae. By a remarkable subsequent development they lose most of their crustacean features in becoming adapted to their special mode of sedentary life.

After moulting several times the first larva changes shape and encloses itself within two tiny shells, which make it look rather like a minute mussel. All this time it has been drifting in the sea among the plankton. Now comes the time for it to settle and take on its adult form. If it falls on to a rock or a stone, or on to a shell or the back of a crab, all is well, but if it falls on sand or mud, or on to seaweed, it dies. The successful larvae settle on their heads, which are provided with a special gland producing a kind of cement. With this the head is firmly fixed to the spot where the animal will spend the rest of its days.

A head complete with eyes and feelers is extremely useful to an animal which moves about, enabling it to avoid danger and to seek out its food. It is less useful to a sedentary animal, and the acorn barnacle's head soon degenerates, only the mouth remaining. The tail, too, so useful to the prawn and the lobster for swimming, is also superflous in a sedentary animal and it, too, degenerates. In the end all that is really left of the barnacle's body is the middle section, the thorax, around which a shell consisting of ten calcareous plates is constructed. Six of these are arranged vertically and fused together to form a complete cover around the sides of the animal, the other four forming a lid which can be opened and closed.

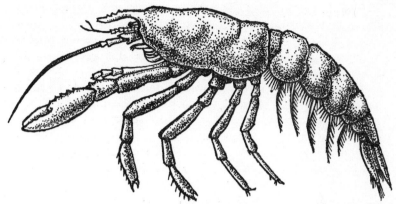

The common prawn

Within its shell the animal, or what is left of it, lies on its back with its legs pointing towards the lid. There are six pairs of these legs, all very thin and curved and each consisting of two branches well supplied with long bristles. It may seem strange that an animal which cannot move should be so well provided with limbs, but the barnacle uses them not for movement but for collecting its food.

When the tide is out, the four lid plates are closed up tightly. If, however, a stone or a shell with attached acorn barnacles is put into water the lid plates will be seen to open. Then out come the curved limbs to commence beating the water. Although it is impossible to see what is happening, they are really trapping minute particles of food suspended in the water and passing them into the shell to the mouth. Thomas Henry Huxley, the eminent nineteenth-century biologist, aptly described the barnacle as a crustacean standing on its head and kicking food into its mouth with its feet.

When the tide goes out and the lid plates are closed some water and a bubble of air are trapped beneath them to enable the barnacle to go on breathing until the tide returns. In hot weather a curious scraping or hissing noise can sometimes be heard around rocks which are covered with acorn barnacles. It is made as thousands of individual barnacles press their lid plates tightly against one another to prevent the water evaporating.

Within its shell plates the acorn barnacle is adequately protected from almost all its potential enemies. Only the dog whelk is really able to prey upon it by boring a hole through the lid plates with its radula. The dog whelk is rather conservative in its feeding habits, apparently preferring to keep to one kind of food so long as supplies last. It will for instance go on feeding on barnacles even though a flourishing mussel colony is developing next door. Only if the barnacle supply gives out will it transfer its attentions to the mussels. If these in turn become seriously depleted it will revert to the barnacles after these have had a chance to recover.

The stalked or ship's barnacle, which is sometimes washed up on the shore attached to driftwood, is a relative of the acorn barnacle. It, too, leads a sedentary life, attached to the bottoms of ships by its head. Although after attachment of the larvae the sense organs degenerate, the head is retained and elongated to form the stalk of the barnacle. The thorax, which forms the functional adult as it does in the acorn barnacle, is enclosed in a shell composed of five separate plates.

The molluscs are as dependent as the crustaceans upon a protective shell, but its construction is completely different. It consists either of a single structure enveloping the whole body (gastropods), or two separate valves hinged together along one edge but also enveloping the whole body (lamellibranchs). The method by which the shell is secreted is the same in the two groups.

The gastropods are the snails, which are widely represented on land, in fresh water and in the sea. The snail's body is soft and relatively featureless. It consists of a hump called the visceral mass which contains all the internal organs and is hidden away within the shell, a thick muscular foot on which it moves, and a small head complete with tentacles and eyes. The foot and head can be protruded from the shell or withdrawn into it as necessity demands. In marine and seashore snails the visceral hump is covered with a loose curtain of tissue called the mantle, which drapes it rather as a bedspread hangs loosely over the sides of a bed.

The function of the mantle is to lay down the shell and add to it continually as the snail grows. The first tiny shell is in fact produced by the mantle of the larva. It is laid down in three distinct layers, the outermost being a thin horny layer consisting of a substance known as conchiolin. Within this is the thickest layer of the shell, consisting of crystalline calcium carbonate. The whole shell is lined with an extremely smooth layer of nacre, or mother of pearl, the material which the pearl oysters use to make pearls. This is also a form of calcium carbonate. The mantle in land snails is much reduced in extent and almost entirely fused with the visceral hump, but it still retains its ability to lay down the shell. In most snails the shell is coiled, and the visceral mass is also coiled to fit into it. There are exceptions, however, notably the limpet, one of the most common of all the seashore snails, in which both the body and the shell remain uncoiled. In sea water there is always plenty of calcium carbonate available for shell production, and in consequence the shells of marine and seashore snails tend to be thick. Land snails, however, find calcium more difficult to come by, and in consequence tend to produce much thinner shells. They tend to be more abundant in chalk and limestone districts than elsewhere.

Many marine and seashore snails carry, attached to the upper surface of the foot, a horny plate called the operculum, which is so placed that when the head and foot are withdrawn into the shell it acts as a door to seal the opening and so protect the occupant. Most land snails do not possess an operculum, but before hibernation they seal the entrance to the shell with a protective layer of dried mucus called the epiphragm.

Even during the summer, if conditions become too dry, a snail may enter into a similar state of suspended animation, called aestivation, in which both heart beat and respiration are slowed down to a small fraction of their normal rates. In exceptional circumstances aestivation has been known to persist without interruption for more than a year, the snail finally emerging apparently none the worse for its prolonged period of inactivity. An African snail sent to the British Museum suddenly started to crawl about after it had been assumed dead and attached to an exhibition card for four years. The emergence took place after the card had been transferred to a room in which the air was damp. Authentic cases are known of uninterrupted aestivation lasting for even longer periods, twenty years being claimed in one case.

The shell of the lamellibranch or bivalve mollusc is very different from that of the gastropod, consisting of two separate valves held together along the dorsal edge by a hinge ligament which tends to keep the valves open. They are closed by the contraction of a pair of adductor muscles, one towards the front and one towards the hind end running across from one valve to the other. The bivalve's body lying between the two valves is covered with a mantle consisting of a right and a left half. Each half is responsible for forming one of the valves. The method by which the mantle lays down the shell is precisely similar to that already described for the gastropod shell, and it has the same three fundamental layers.

The adductor muscles are extremely powerful, and few enemies are able to open a bivalve shell against their determined contraction. The principal enemies of the marine and seashore lamellibranchs generally are the starfish (see Chapter 5) and the various kinds of carnivorous snails.

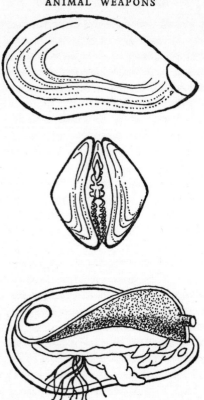

Three views of the common mussel. Top: the complete shell viewed from the right side (hind end to the left). Middle: view from rear showing upper exhalant and lower inhalant openings. Below: view from right side with right valve removed and mantle turned back to reveal the curtain-like gills, the muscular foot and the byssus threads by which the mussel anchors itself to the rocks

The two most valuable kinds of bivalve molluscs are the edible oysters and the pearl oysters. Edible oysters all belong to the genus *Ostrea*, and are widespread in the coastal waters of Europe and North America. Pearl oysters are all species of *Margaritifer*, and are mostly found in warmer eastern waters. The feature which distinguishes them from most other bivalves is that the inner layer of the shell is much thicker, and iridescent. It can be separated from the remainder of the shell to provide the mother-of-pearl of commerce, which is used to make buttons and other small objects. The pearl itself is just a separate piece of mother-of-pearl, usually spherical in shape and found lying between the mantle and the shell, and not generally fixed to the shell.

Pearls represent an ingenious method used by the pearl oysters to minimise the irritation caused by foreign bodies trapped within their shell by giving them a smooth coating. Such particles may become lodged within the tissue of the mantle or between it and the inner surface of the shell. The mantle reacts by covering the particle with a smooth layer of mother-of-pearl, the end result usually being spherical. Some pearls are connected at one point to the shell, and these blister pearls, as they are called, are of little value. They can however be sawn off and used in cheap jewellery.

Many other bivalves produce pearls, but these are of no commerical value.

Often the nucleus of a pearl is the egg or larva of a parasite, and sometimes an oyster's own egg may go astray and become the starting point for the formation of a pearl. Tiny grains of sand or other similar material can also initiate pearl production. Of course only a small proportion of pearl oysters produce pearls. Fewer than one in every hundred in fact contains a pearl even when fully grown, and only a small proportion of these pearls has any commercial value.

It was inevitable, once the true nature of pearls became known, that attempts should be made to introduce foreign particles into pearl oysters in the hope of stimulating them to produce pearls. The main difficulties were to evolve a technique for opening the oysters without damaging them, and to find particles which the oysters would not reject. Success was finally achieved in Japan after many years of intensive experiment. It was found that the only thing not rejected by the oysters when inserted between the mantle and the shell was a tiny piece of mother-of-pearl wrapped in a tiny bag made from fresh mantle tissue.

Pearls produced by oysters in response to this artificial stimulus are known as cultured pearls to distinguish them from the pearls which result from a naturally occurring stimulus. They are, however, true pearls, differing only from the so-called natural pearls in that the nucleus is a piece of mother-of-pearl and not a grain of sand or a minute egg or larva.

Although there are no relatives of the pearl oysters living in the seas of northern Europe, some fast-flowing Scottish rivers do contain the so-called pearl mussel, *Margaritifer margaritifer*, which as the name suggests is more closely related to the pearl oysters than it is to typical mussels. Pearls in these mussels are formed in exactly the same way as in the pearl oyster. British pearl fisheries were famous even in Roman times, and even as late as the middle of the eighteenth century considerable profits were being made from pearl fisheries in certain of the Scottish rivers.

From the structural point of view the most remarkable shell in all nature is that produced by the sea urchin. If we consider the starfish as a remarkable animal because of its unusual structure, we must regard the sea urchin as being really revolutionary. At first sight there may seem to be little resemblance between the flat starfish with its prominent arms and the prickly ball which is the sea urchin. Yet really the sea urchin may be seen as the result of a drastic experiment with the typical starfish structure. The structure of a sea urchin can best be understood if we imagine the five arms of a starfish turned upward and inward so that the tips meet above its body with the five spaces between filled in, the whole forming a hollow ball.

The long spines of the sea urchin are comparable with the much shorter spines of the starfish, while between them there are numerous pincer organs. A careful examination will show that, starting from near the mouth opening on the lower side, five double rows of tube feet run nearly up to the top of the ball. The sea urchin uses these in the same way as the starfish to glide along the sea bed. If it falls it will not matter how because some of the tube feet will be near the ground, and it will therefore be able to move and right itself.

The crowning glory of the sea urchin's structure is its globular shell or test, normally obscured by the multitude of spines, tube feet and pincer organs. Sometimes the test of a dead urchin is washed up on the beach denuded of all its appendages, and then its wonderful construction can be seen. It consists of hundreds of tiny plates fitting accurately together. In life it is covered with a thin layer of skin from which the various appendages grow, so that it is an internal and not an external skeleton. It represents a modification of the loose skeleton of the starfish, the plates having grown and fused together. As the sea urchin grows so its test is increased in size through an increase in the area of each individual plate, calcareous material being deposited round the edges by the skin.

The wonderful construction of the sea urchin's test excited the admiration of the early naturalists. Gosse, in his *Year at the Shore*, had this to say of it:

A globular hollow box has to be made, of some three inches in diameter, the walls of which shall be scarcely thicker than a wafer, formed of unyielding limestone, yet fitted to hold the soft tender parts of an animal which quite fill the concavity of all ages. But in infancy the animal . . . is not so big as a pea; and it has to grow till it attains its adult dimensions. The box is never cast off, and replaced by a new one; the same box must hold the infant and the veteran urchin. The limestone . . . can only grow by being deposited. . . . The box is not made in one piece, nor in ten, nor in a hundred; six hundred pieces go to make up the hollow case; all so accurately fitted together that the perfect symmetry of the outline is not broken; and yet, thin as their substance is, they retain their relative position with unchanging exactness, and the slight brittle box possesses all the requisite strength and firmness.

CHAPTER 4

Spines for Offence and Defence

SPINES have been developed as offensive and defensive weapons in a number of different animal groups, but they are particularly common among fishes. Even in Britain we have an extremely poisonous shore fish, the lesser weever, *Trachinus vipera*, which is able to wriggle into the sand with the help of its pectoral fins. Here it lies buried just beneath the surface with only the top of the head, including the mouth and the eyes, and the tips of the spines of the dorsal fins, protruding above the surface.

The lesser weever feeds on crustacea, especially shrimps, and occurs mainly on sandy shores where shrimps are plentiful. It is often captured in shrimpers' nets. There are spines on the top of the head, on the dorsal fins, and one on each gill cover. Each spine is grooved, and into each groove opens a poison gland. The eyes and the mouth point upwards to enable them to remain just above the surface when the rest of the body is buried. If held in the hand the weever tries to strike with its spines by vigorous lateral movements of its body. Anyone who goes shrimping in bare feet runs the risk of being poisoned by the lesser weever, because they tend to be most numerous where there are plenty of shrimps. Gosse gives a variety of alternative names for the weever, mostly originating from fishermen, such as sting fish, sting bull, sea cat and sea dragon. He also says that the name weever is a corruption from the French, 'who call it Vive, from the length of time which the fish will *live* out of its native element'.

The lesser weever seldom exceeds six inches in length. Another species, the greater weever, *Trachinus draco*, can grow to twice this length, but this is really a species belonging to the offshore waters, and is seldom encountered on shore.

Two other fish armed with poison spines and found in inshore waters are the father lasher, *Cottus scorpius*, and the long-spined sea scorpion, *Cottus bubalis*. The father lasher is the larger of the two related species, sometimes attaining a length of six feet, and since its venom is as virulent as that of the weever it is certainly a dangerous fish. The long-spined sea scorpion seldom exceeds twelve inches in length. Neither has any spines on its fins, but each gill-cover is armed with several spines, each with its own poison gland. Small but still dangerous specimens of the father lasher can often be found in rock pools but, like the weever, they should be very carefully handled if caught, for they will certainly try to wriggle into a position for striking with their spines.

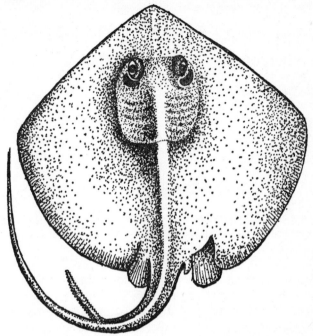

The sting ray has a long poisonous serrated spine or 'sting' growing from about midway along its thin whip-like tail

Among the skates and rays there is one group known as the sting rays on account of their poisonous spine or 'sting'. The tail of a sting ray is particularly thin even for a member of a group in which the tail is never very broad, and it lacks the two dorsal fins towards the end of the tail which all other members of the group possess. The poisonous spine replaces them. This is long, serrated and very sharp, and is capable of making a deep jagged wound. Two grooves run throughout its length and along them lie the glands which secrete a venom sufficiently potent to kill a man. Like some snake venoms it acts on the nervous system. The spine, which may grow to a length of up to fifteen inches, is periodically shed and replaced by a new one which has already been developing behind it. Sometimes three spines in different stages of development may be present at the same time. The sting ray's tail is extremely mobile, making the fish dangerous to handle, for it will strike home with great rapidity. Sting rays are common and widespread, especially in tropical and subtropical waters, but one species, *Trygon pastinaca*, occurs in British waters as well as throughout the Atlantic and Indian Oceans and as far east as Japan.

The body of the porcupine fish is covered with spines, and is capable of swelling up if danger threatens, making it virtually impossible for any larger enemy to swallow

No animal uses its spines in defence more unusually than the porcupine globe fish, *Diodon hystrix*. This fish, widely distributed in the warmer parts of the Atlantic, Indian and Pacific Oceans, has a rather elongated cylindrical body covered all over with sharp spines. These lie on the surface pointing backwards, in which position their effectiveness as weapons is minimal. If the fish feels itself threatened, however, it can swallow enormous quantities of water, or air if it comes to the surface, which has the effect of turning the whole body into the shape of a globe, and of causing the spines to stand out vertically from the surface. In this condition the fish is virtually impossible to swallow, at least without causing grave internal damage to any predator misguided enough to do so. When danger is passed the air is expelled and the fish resumes its normal activities.

The air which is taken in does not go into the stomach, but into a series of sacs opening ventrally from the gullet into the lower part of the body. The fish thus floats with its back downwards, being able to right itself only when it finally expels the air.

Related to the porcupine fish are the puffer fish, species of the genus *Tetrodon*. They are similar in appearance and have the same extraordinary ability to swallow air to inflate their bodies when threatened.

Their spines are shorter, but their enemies find them still virtually impossible to swallow. Some species live in fresh water in Africa and in South America.

If spines are on the whole defensive rather than offensive weapons, there is one type of spine which is undoubtedly offensive in purpose, and this is the sword of the swordfish. Swordfish together with spearfish and tunnies are all large members of the mackerel family, fish which are perfectly streamlined for swimming through the water at great speed. Swordfish are widespread in the surface waters of seas and oceans in many parts of the world, and they are extremely savage. The sword is a long bony prolongation of the upper jaw. As the swordfish rushes among shoals of surface-swimming fish the sharp sword probably kills

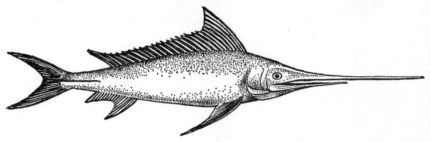

The formidable sword of the swordfish is really a long bony prolongation
of the upper jaw

many of them, which can then be gathered up at leisure. Swordfish are even credited with attacking whales and cutting large pieces out of their sides, and in the days of wooden ships these were often attacked, the sword sinking deep into the wood. To escape it was necessary for the fish to break off its sword. In such attacks large specimens might plunge their swords considerable depths into the wood. The Natural History Museum in London has a piece of ship's timber into which a swordfish's sword has penetrated twenty-two inches. Members of the swordfish–tunny family provide some of the world's most spectacular sporting fish for the big-game fisherman. They have been immortalised by Ernest Hemingway in his famous book *The Old Man and the Sea*.

Although superficially similar, in that they also have an offensive weapon formed from a prolongation of the upper jaw, the sawfishes are not at all closely related to the swordfishes. The sawfish is in fact a modified shark, its skeleton being made of cartilage and not of bone. The sword of the swordfish has the shape of a spear, but the saw of the sawfish is a flattened and somewhat tapering blade in which the cartilage is calcified for added strength. Along each side it is armed with a row of sharp teeth. In large specimens the saw may be as much as six feet in length with a width of up to one foot as it leaves the head. Like the swordfish the sawfish is a savage predator, swimming into shoals of fish with powerful side-to-side movements of its saw, killing large numbers of them to gather up at its leisure. Specimens weighing more than 5,000 lb have been caught on rod and line by big game fishermen in the waters around the West Indies.

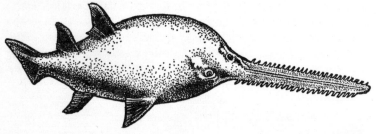

The saw of the sawfish is an extension of the upper jaw. It is made of cartilage, unlike the bony sword of the swordfish; the sawfish is a relative of the shark

Among mammals the hedgehog and the porcupines have adopted spines as their principal method of defence against their enemies. The spine of a hedgehog is a highly modified hair produced from a follicle in the skin similar in structure to a normal hair follicle. The sharp tip of the spine is solid, but the shaft contains air-filled compartments separated by thin cross plates which serve to give it added strength. Spines occur only on the upper surface of the body, the under surface being covered with normal hair.

Coupled with the hedgehog's ability to roll itself into a ball when danger threatens, the spines provide a most effective method of protection. The confidence they have in the protection afforded by their spines when they roll up, however, probably accounts for the large numbers of hedgehogs killed on the roads. Although they can move quite fast and should normally have plenty of time to run out of danger when they are picked up in a car's headlights, they curl into a ball in the middle of the road instead.

Hedgehog spines also serve another protective function. Hedgehogs are great climbers, and will scale a six-foot fence of wire netting with the greatest of ease, usually dropping from the top to the ground on the other side in the rolled-up position, so that the spines act as shock absorbers.

There is, however, one great disadvantage in having a skin full of spines. It cannot be groomed as most mammals groom their fur, using their paws as combs and sometimes their tongues as brushes. As a consequence it makes a wonderful hideout for an astounding variety of fleas and mites, which the hedgehog is powerless to disturb.

The hedgehog is a member of the Insectivora, and is therefore related to the moles and the shrews. As their group name suggests, they feed on insects and other small animals. The only other mammals to provide themselves with protective spines, the porcupines, are rodents, and as such they are mainly vegetarian. There are two distinct groups of porcupines, one found in the New World and one in the Old. The best known of them all is also the largest, the crested porcupine, *Hystrix cristata*, which is widely distributed in Africa. The quills, as the spines of the porcupine are called, are of two kinds, long, slender and flexible quills which overlie and mainly conceal the shorter stout quills. All are marked with broad rings of black and white, the tips being always white.

Although porcupines have no reason to attack other animals, their quills do provide them with a considerable measure of protection against most potential predators. If alarmed they produce a peculiar rattling noise by shaking their quills. This may serve both to warn off the enemies and to alert neighbouring porcupines to the approach of danger. In earlier times there was a belief that porcupines could eject their quills at any enemy approaching from behind. This would indeed constitute a wonderful defence mechanism, but is unfortunately one which the porcupine does not possess. It will however run swiftly backwards at an approaching enemy and make painful contact unless quick avoiding action is taken.

Most of the New World procupines are tree dwellers, and all are distinguished from their Old World relatives by their quills. These are much shorter and thinner but in one respect more efficient. Towards their tips are tiny barbs, and these make it difficult to extract the quills once they are embedded. Normally the quills lie backwards along the skin, but as soon as the animal feels itself threatened muscular action brings them erect. Like the Old World porcupines they, too, will turn their backs on an enemy and then back smartly into it, leaving its nose and face covered with painfully embedded quills.

CHAPTER 5

Suckers

SUCKERS are not a general weapon in the animal kingdom, but there are a few groups of animals which have perfected the art of using them in the capture of their prey, and in these groups the suckers have become as efficient as any other method of attack and defence.

No animals use suckers more efficiently and effectively than the starfish. These, along with the sea urchins and sea cucumbers, constitute the Echinoderms or spiny-skinned animals, nature's one successful experiment in producing complex animals built on a radial or circular plan, as distinct from the bilateral or fore-and-aft plan to which the remainder of the higher animal groups conform. The only other successful animals built on the radial plan are the Coelenterates, the lowly sea-anemones and jelly-fish.

The common starfish, which is often left stranded on the beach by the receding tide, will serve as a good introduction to the group. It consists of a small central body or disc from which grow five tapering arms. These arms are much more than appendages for locomotion. There is not sufficient room in the small central disc for all the necessary

The central disc of a sunstar showing twelve double rows of tube feet
suckers

internal organs, so the arms provide room for some of them, housing the reproductive system and part of the digestive system.

If you pick up the starfish you will notice that it has a soft, almost flabby, body, but the skin is rough. This skin in fact plays an important part in the life of the animal, and is covered with numerous tiny outgrowths. Many of these are short, blunt spines which are based on tiny calcareous plates embedded in the skin and forming a loose skeleton. There is no internal provision for breathing, and the other outgrowths provide for respiration. These are the skin gills, tiny transparent projections through which the necessary exchange of gases takes place. A lens or a microscope would reveal a third set of skin structures, each like a tiny pair of pincers on a long flexible stalk scattered all over the skin between the spines and the gills. These are the pedicellariae, which are used to keep the skin clean by picking off any stray particles falling on it.

When you watch a starfish moving about on the bottom of a rock pool, it seems to glide slowly along without moving its body. If you turn it over you will discover the secret of its locomotion. A groove runs right along the underside of each arm from the central disc to the tip. On either side of this groove there is a row of small tube feet each ending in a flat disc which can be used as a sucker. These tube feet are hollow and open into a canal which is filled with water and runs along the whole length of the arm. Their movements are controlled by pumping water into and out of them from the canal. The five canals open into a central disc, and this in turn opens to the outside through a porous plate called the madreporite, which is on one side of the upper surface of the disc.

The starfish cannot move along very fast on its tube feet, which are pushed forward in turn in the direction the animal is going and then fixed by their suckers. Contraction of the feet then pulls the body along a little way, and the process is repeated. In attaching a tube foot, the disc is placed flat on the surface and then the central portion is withdrawn to create a vacuum. Tube feet are capable of gripping quite tightly, with a force equal to about 25 lb to the square inch, which is quite sufficient to enable the animal to climb a vertical rock face. The vacuum can account for only part of the adhesive force, since it cannot exceed atmospheric pressure, which is about 15 lb to the square inch. The rest is accounted for by a sticky mucus produced by special glands at the end of the foot and passed out over the disc.

If you turn the starfish on its back in water you will be able to see the tube feet in action. First the tip of one arm is turned under so that its outer tube feet can grip the sand or rock. Other arms are gradually brought into use in the same way, until a sufficient grip is obtained for the whole body to be dragged over so that it is once again right side up.

The starfish has no complex sense organs, but at the tip of each arm there is a single tube foot which has become drastically modified to form an eyespot sensitive to light. It is usually carried upturned, and its surface is covered with minute cups lined with sensitive cells. The tube foot next to it, though not noticeably modified in structure, is believed to be sensitive to smell.

The feeding habits of the starfish are as remarkable as its structure. It has no teeth or jaws, and its mouth is only a fleshy opening in the centre of the underside of the body leading into the large stomach which nearly fills the central disc. Nor has it any offensive weapons except its tube feet and the rather weak muscles of its arms. Yet it is an exclusively carnivorous animal, feeding on shellfish and able to overcome oysters and mussels as large as itself. Small shellfish, including young oysters and mussels, are passed whole through the mouth into the stomach, where the digestive juices first kill and then digest them. Afterwards the empty shells are cast out through the mouth.

Large oysters and mussels, however, are much too big to go through the mouth, and the starfish digests these outside its body. Hunching itself over the oyster or mussel, it grips the two valves of the shell with its tube feet and pulls. For a long time nothing happens, because the adductor muscles closing the valves are much more powerful than the starfish muscles. They are, however, more easily tired, and after some time, perhaps an hour or two, they begin to weaken, and the starfish is able to force the valves slowly apart.

Then a surprising thing happens. The starfish turns its stomach inside-out through its mouth over the exposed body of the oyster or mussel, and pours digestive juices on to it. The products of digestion are slowly absorbed through the wall of the stomach as digestion proceeds.

Living always on the sea bed the starfish is liable to get its arms caught under stones rolled by the waves. Like the crab it can free itself by amputating the trapped arms and growing new ones. It has, in fact, great powers of regeneration. Sometimes only one arm and a portion of the central disc can be torn away, but even from this remnant a complete starfish can be regenerated.

Large numbers of starfish are often found on oyster and mussel beds, where they can become a major plague. Before their powers of regeneration were known oyster fishermen, infuriated by the damage they caused, used to take any starfish which came up in the dredge and pull it to pieces before throwing it back into the water, little realising that in doing so they were helping their enemies to multiply.

One species of starfish is causing great concern currently in Australia and in other parts of the Pacific, where it has increased to plague proportions in recent years. The crown of thorns starfish, *Acanthaster planci*, is one of the world's largest, measuring up to two feet across and having between fifteen and seventeen arms instead of the usual five. The spines on its upper surface, instead of being short and blunt, are up to two inches in length and sharp, and are capable of causing an extremely painful wound if they penetrate the skin. They are believed to inject a poison, and can in exceptional cases result in the death of the injured person.

The principal food of the crown of thorns consists of coral polyps, whose activities result in the formation of the coral reefs which are such a feature of Pacific islands. Coral polyps are coelenterates related to sea-anemones, but unlike these they live in vast colonies, and each polyp secretes around its base a calcareous cup. As each generation of polyps dies the members of the succeeding generation secrete their cups on the top of those of their predecessors, and in this way a solid calcareous reef is gradually formed.

Almost every Pacific island is surrounded by its coral reef, but the largest and most famous is the Great Barrier Reef, which extends for 1,200 miles down the east coast of Australia, and consists of something like 2,500 separate but adjacent reefs.

Each starfish is known to be capable of killing every single coral polyp over an area of two square feet each day, its method of feeding being to evert its stomach over the polyps and digest them in the same way as any other starfish will digest a mussel or oyster which it has succeeded in opening. The terrifying aspect of the crown of thorns is the vast number which exists today. Some authorities believe that off the island of Guam since the last war as much as 98 per cent of a thirty-mile stretch of coral off one side of the island may have been destroyed. Already it is estimated that 10 per cent of the Great Barrier Reef has also been virtually destroyed. Once the polyps have been destroyed the reef is exposed to the action of the waves and can soon disintegrate.

Australian scientists are carrying out urgent investigations into possible methods of destroying the starfish. Unfortunately, as we have already seen, they are not easily killed, and as they can each produce up to twenty million eggs annually, even a few survivors might well be capable of quickly repopulating an area from which the majority of adults had been eliminated. To give some idea of the vast numbers involved a recent expedition to the Barrier Reef by a party of scientists from Queensland University caught 750 specimens from one hundred square yards of reef in the space of two hours.

Like the starfish, the octopus is also a creature endowed with arms provided with numerous suckers which play an essential part in capturing and dealing with its prey. No one lacking knowledge of its evolutionary history would think of relating the octopus to the snail or the winkle. Yet it is indeed a mollusc, and its remote ancestors possessed a coiled shell and a muscular foot on which they were able to glide along over rock surfaces. In the course of time the foot became modified to form eight tentacles or arms surrounding the mouth, while the shell became progressively reduced in size until it was finally lost altogether.

The arms of the common octopus are wonderful structures. They are broad where they leave the body and taper to fine flexible ends, the broad bases being connected by a membrane. All along the underside of each arm there is a double row of suckers, graded in size from an inch or more in diameter at the base to about one-sixteenth of an inch at the extreme tip. Each sucker consists of a ring of muscle with a fleshy disc in the centre. When the arm is used to grip an object the suckers are first pressed flat on to it, and then the fleshy disc is withdrawn by muscular action to form a vacuum, working in the same way as a suction disc. With all its suckers an octopus has considerable gripping power at its command.

Crabs and lobsters are its favourite food, and it is for these that it goes hunting at night, rising into the water and descending like a cloud over any unfortunate crab it encounters. Even when hiding in its lair during the daytime it remains on the alert for any unsuspecting crab which may happen to pass, flicking out one of its arms to touch the crab lightly as soon as it comes within reach. Then a curious thing happens. The crab raises itself on its legs and holds up its claws, a typical defensive attitude, as though it is going to attack the octopus arm. But that is as far as its defensive instincts take it, for it appears to be in some way hypnotised by the octopus, which without further trouble is able to drag it in and tuck it away in the folds of its arm webs.

The captured crab may be kept alive for some time while others are collected. One octopus was observed to collect no fewer than seventeen crabs before finally settling down to its meal. To get at the crab meat it pulls off the arms and legs, using the flexible ends of its arms to extract it and pass it into its mouth. An octopus lair can sometimes be discovered by the heap of empty crab shells lying around the entrance.

Lobsters are more difficult for the octopus to catch than crabs, because they do not appear to be afraid of it. The danger to the octopus is of course the lobster's claws, and the first aim of the octopus is to get a firm grip on these with its suckers. Once it has succeeded the lobster is vanquished, but a prolonged battle of wits may occur before a really big lobster is overpowered.

The only close relatives of the octopus are the ten-armed squids and cuttlefish. They have two very long arms or tentacles with which they catch their prey, as well as eight shorter arms which can be used to deal with the prey once it has been captured. The tentacles have suckers only on their thickened club-shaped tips; when not in use, they can be withdrawn into pouches at the sides of the head. Squid suckers, unlike those of the octopus, are borne on short stalks, and each has a horny, detachable rim which may be toothed.

Squids and cuttlefish lead a much more active life than the octopus, swimming in the open seas, and their bodies are streamlined. Along the sides of the body a pair of flat stabilising fins grows out. They are gregarious animals, and often swim in vast shoals. While most squids and cuttlefish are quite small, there are some formidable deep-sea monster squids, the largest of which may attain a length, including the tentacles, of fifty feet or more. These giant squids are widely distributed in the open oceans, but are seldom encountered, though dead specimens are occasionally washed up on the shore, usually in an advanced state of decay.

The club-shaped end of one of the long tentacles of a cuttle fish showing the rimmed suckers with which it is so plentifully supplied

They are powerful creatures, able to inflict damage on the large cachalot or sperm whales. Large squids are the favourite diet of these sixty-foot whales, but with their formidable suckers they are not apparently overpowered without a struggle, and the huge head and jaws of the whales often show numerous large scars made by the suckers.

A number of different kinds of fish are provided with suckers, but only in the lampreys are they specifically used as weapons of attack. The lampreys and hag-fishes together form the most primitive group of vertebrates, the Cyclostomata, or jawless fishes. Instead of jaws adult lampreys are provided with a well-developed round sucker containing numerous horny teeth. The round mouth, which opens in the middle of the sucker, has a muscular tongue which is also well armed with strong teeth. Whenever food is required the lamprey seeks out a suitable fish as victim, and attaches its suctorial mouth almost anywhere on the fish's body. With its tongue it then proceeds to rasp away at the fish's skin until it has excavated a shallow wound, through which it sucks up both blood and flesh. The lamprey remains attached to its victim only so long as it is feeding. When it has absorbed sufficient for its present needs it relinquishes its hold and swims away. In rivers and lakes where lampreys exist in considerable numbers fish are often caught showing the wounds from several separate lamprey attacks.

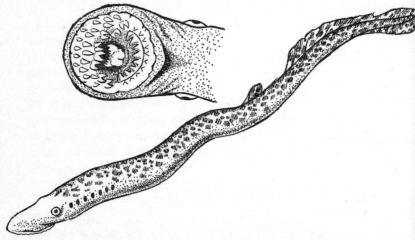

Lamprey and view of the circular toothed sucker surrounding the mouth

The largest of the small number of different lamprey species is the so-called sea lamprey, *Petromyzon marinus*, which is widespread both in Europe and in North America. Full-grown adults measure about three feet in length. Like the salmon, the adult sea lamprey lives most of its adult life in the sea, but ascends rivers at the approach of the breeding season to spawn in fresh water. The males arrive first and begin preparing nests – shallow depressions in the river-bed surrounded by stones, the fish using their suckers to place these stones in position. After mating the eggs are covered by the body movements of the parents and left to hatch. Spawning is the lampreys' last function; soon afterwards they die, apparently exhausted by the effort.

The lamprey larvae which result remain in the river for a year or two, during which time they grow from about one-third of an inch to about six inches long. All this time they live buried in the mud on the river-bed. They have no suckers, and feed on minute organisms and particles which they filter out of the water current taken in through the mouth to pass over their gills. When metamorphosis occurs the changes take place quickly, the most important of these from our point of view being the suctorial mouth and tongue, both armed with horny teeth.

As soon as metamorphosis occurs the young adult lampreys make their way down stream to the sea, only returning after a number of years when it comes their turn to breed.

Lampreys were at one time much more common in many British rivers than they are today, and large numbers used to be caught for eating when they returned from the sea to spawn. Many people in fact regarded them as a delicacy. Most schoolboys remember that Henry I is said to have died from 'a surfeit of lampreys'. Pollution of rivers in modern times may well have been the cause of the great reduction in numbers which has certainly occurred.

In the Great Lakes of North America the sea lamprey has become the principal enemy both of the fish which live in the lakes and the commercial fishermen whose livelihood depends upon them. A glance at the map of North America will show that between the sea and the Great Lakes the Niagara Falls constitute a barrier which one might think would be completely impassable to any fish, let alone such a weak swimmer as the lamprey. Yet in 1921 the authorities received a shock when a Canadian fisherman found in his catch a large lake trout with a lamprey firmly attached by its sucker mouth to its side. This was the first piece of evidence that the sea lamprey had somehow succeeded in penetrating the fresh waters above Niagara.

It is now believed that the first lamprey invaders came in from Lake Ontario, which is below Niagara, through the Welland Canal which links this lake with Lake Erie, which is above the falls. They may have travelled attached to the bottoms of ships using the canal. It is known that lampreys do sometimes travel by this method.

Once established in the lakes it was no longer possible for them to travel down to the sea in large numbers after metamorphosis, but they seem to have had no difficulty in adjusting their behaviour pattern to suit their new conditions. Today they treat the lakes as they would the sea, spending their adult lives existing on the fish in them and migrating up the streams feeding the lakes to spawn. The larvae remain in these streams, the young lampreys swimming down to the lakes immediately after metamorphosis.

The spread of the lampreys through the Great Lakes has been spectacular. By about 1936 they had become firmly established in Lake Huron, and their presence in this lake soon proved disastrous to the fishing industry. For the previous forty years U.S. fishermen had maintained a steady annual catch of some 1,700,000 lb of trout without difficulty. From that year, however, there was a steady decline, until by 1948 the total catch was less than 5,000 lb. From 1940 the Canadian fishermen experienced a similar decline, their catch being reduced from a previous annual average of 4,000,000 lb to 40,000 lb in little more than ten years. Today trout are virtually absent from Huron. Subsequently the lampreys found their way first into Lake Michigan and finally reached Lake Superior, where the same catastrophic story is being repeated. In any of the lakes now a trout which has not been attacked by lampreys at least once is a rarity. Curiously, although it was the first lake to be colonised by the blood-sucking invaders, Erie has suffered less than the others, and still retains a reasonable trout population. It is possible that some of the decline has been due to a rapid increase in pollution in the trout lakes which has been taking place during the same period.

In contrast to all the previous users of suckers, which employ them for aggressive purposes, the remora uses its sucker as a means of protection. The remora is a relatively small marine fish a foot or two in length. It is seldom found swimming free in the sea, although it is widespread and common in many of the warmer waters of the world. Almost invariably it is found firmly attached to some larger fish, often a shark, and for this reason it is sometimes known as the shark-sucker.

When it is quite small it is similar in general appearance to any other fish, but as it grows its dorsal fin gradually flattens, spreading outwards over its shoulders and forwards over its head until it has changed into a large corrugated sucker which looks somewhat like the sole of a tennis shoe. With this extremely efficient sucker it attaches itself beneath its partner. Only when its partner is feeding will it detach itself, and then it helps to eat the food which has been caught. Before the meal is quite finished it attaches itself again in readiness for departure. Its sucker provides it with complete protection against potential enemies, for no fish is going to attack it while it is attached to such a formidable partner as a shark. It is also relieved of the necessity of searching for its own food.

Besides sharks and other fish, the remora will also fix itself to large turtles, porpoises, sea-cows and even to ships. Its habits have been known for a very long time. The ancient Greeks and Romans believed that a number of sucker fish on the bottom of a ship could slow it down or even stop it. Since the largest kind grow to only about three feet in length, it seems unlikely that they could affect a vessel's speed.

The remora sucker is extremely efficient and powerful. It is said that if you try to pull the fish away from the sides of the glass tank to which it has attached itself, it will allow the sucker to be torn away from its body rather than loosen its grip. Because of its ability to fix itself so firmly to other animals the remora has been used for hundreds and maybe for thousands of years for catching fish and other animals which live in the sea. For this purpose it is fitted with a rope harness attached to a long line, and then thrown overboard from the fishing boat. It will attach itself to the first large fish it sees, for a remora is apparently ill at ease if it is not fixed to a partner. Once attached it will hold on grimly, pulled one way by the fish and the other way by the rope. This is drawn in towards the boat until both fish are safely hauled aboard. The remora will seldom let go of the catch before it can be brought alongside.

The favourite quarry for these remora fishermen are turtles, to which the remora will adhere as readily as it will to any fish. It is held in the boat until a turtle is sighted, when it will be sent off after it. Often the turtle is too big to be hauled in to the boat's side, and instead it dives down to the sea-bed. But the remora retains its grip and is carried down with it. Overboard goes one of the fishermen, following the rope attached to the fish until it leads him to the turtle. He then ties a strong rope to it so that the fishermen in the boat can haul it up to the surface.

It seems strange that so many people in widely separated parts of the world should all have adopted this method of fishing. It is practised in the West Indies, Australia, Malaya, China, Japan and many other parts of the Far East. Was it first discovered by one group of people, who then taught the others? This seems unlikely. It is more probable that during the course of time each of these races discovered the method for themselves.

CHAPTER 6

Animal Projectiles

DESPITE the immense variety of offensive and defensive weapons employed throughout the animal kingdom, capturing prey by shooting it down might seem to be the one human weapon which it would be impossible for an animal to evolve. There is, however, one kind of fish, the archer fish, which has developed into an extremely accomplished shot, its 'bullets' being small drops of water aimed with extreme accuracy and remarkable power.

More than 200 years ago early travellers returning from the Far East brought back stories of a small fish which swam about just beneath the surface of the water and was able to shoot down insects resting on overhanging leaves and branches by accurate bombardment with drops of water. No one at the time believed them, but later travellers repeated these stories. It is only during the past few decades that these archer fish have been fully investigated and the stories of the early travellers confirmed.

The archer fish comprise six different species of *Toxotes*, which live in brackish water in coastal areas from India to the Philippines and as far south as Australia. The largest and best known is *Toxotes jaculatrix*, which grows to a length of about ten inches, none of the other species exceeding eight inches in length.

Despite their small size they are capable of shooting with uncanny accuracy for a distance of several feet above the surface of the water. The water drops hit the resting insects with considerable force, so that they drop into the water, when of course the fish snap them up immediately.

Observers found that up to a distance of four feet away the fish virtually never missed. The very best shots were able to send the drops of water as much as twelve feet above the surface. On more than one occasion a man smoking on a veranda overlooking water in which archer fish were living has had his cigarette extinguished by well-directed salvos. One fish was observed to shoot down a small lizard which was sunning itself on a leaf a few inches above the water, but this was probably too large a prey to be swallowed.

In 1935 C. W. Coates, curator of the New York Aquarium, acquired two specimens of *Toxotes jaculatrix* in order to carry out further investigations under aquarium conditions. Within a few days they were shooting down spiders, cockroaches and other insects placed on suitable positions above the water surface. During these experiments Coates found that the archer fish showed considerable intelligence. When they were offered a spider fixed to the end of a stick so that it could not be shot down they soon gave up, and refused to shoot at anything else until they became really hungry.

With this remarkable ability one might expect to find some extreme modification of the mouth in these archer fish. In fact detailed examination has shown that the tongue, which in most fish is fastened down firmly to the floor of the mouth, is looser than normal, enabling it to be pressed up to the roof of the mouth, which has a straight groove running forwards. This groove and the tongue together form a tube which can be used rather like a peashooter to project the drops of water. In firing the gill covers are pressed smartly inwards, so that water is sent through the tube under considerable pressure.

This anatomical information does not in itself explain the extreme accuracy achieved by the archer fish, only the power of its shooting. When it shoots, its eyes are below the surface of the water, so that in taking aim it must take account of the bending of the light. Everyone knows that a stick looks bent in the middle when half of it is in water. The lower half of the stick is thus not where it appears to be. In the same way the insect on the leaf is not where the fish sees it. It must therefore make the necessary adjustment to its aim, shooting the drops where the insect is, and not at the spot where it appears to be. How it achieves this adjustment remains a mystery. Again, the surface of the water may be choppy, but the archer fish is able to make allowance for this as well.

Young archer fish begin to practise the art of shooting even when they are only about an inch long, but as the drops are projected only two or three inches they provide the young fish with no food. Until they have grown large enough to project much farther they have to rely upon small creatures living in the water.

It is interesting now to examine the first published account of the activities of the archer fish, and to realise how complete and accurate it was. It appeared in no less authentic a source than the Philosophical Transactions of the Royal Society of London, the world's premier scientific society, in the year 1765. The paper, which dealt with the 'jaculator or shooting fish', describes it as follows:

It frequents the shores and sides of the sea and rivers, in search of food. When it spies a fly sitting on the plants that grow in shallow water it swims on to the distance of four, five or six feet, and then, with surprising dexterity, it ejects out of its tubular mouth a single drop of water, which never fails in striking the fly into the sea, where it soon becomes its prey.

The author of the paper was in fact reporting the findings of the governor of a hospital in Batavia, who had made a detailed study of the fish. The account continues:

> The relation of this uncommon action of this cunning fish raised the governor's curiosity; though it came well attested, yet he was determined, if possible, to be convinced of the truth, by ocular demonstration. For that purpose he ordered a large wide tun to be filled with sea-water; then had some of these caught, and put into it, which was changed every other day. In a while, they seemed reconciled to their confinement; then he determined to try the experiment. A slender stick, with a fly pinned on at its end, was placed in such a direction, on the side of the vessel, as the fish could strike it. It was with inexpressible delight, that he daily saw these fish exercising their skill in shooting at the fly with amazing dexterity, and never missed the mark.

In the history of zoology it is not unusual for an early discovery to have become completely forgotten, hidden away in some scientific journal, to be rediscovered at some much later date. The classic example is the work of Mendel on plant breeding which, when it was rediscovered, led to the foundation of the modern science of genetics.

But this account of the archer fish was neither lost nor ignored. One after the other, for well over a hundred years, leading authorities on the fishes of south-east Asia denied the archer fish's ability. For example Dr Francis Day, a noted authority who devoted more than a quarter of a century to the study of the fishes of the region and published many volumes still recognised today for their general accuracy, dismissed the alleged abilities of *Toxotes* in a book written in 1889 in two sentences: 'It is stated in some works that these wide-mouthed fishes shoot insects with a drop of water in Batavia. Bleeker (an earlier authority) observed that he never witnessed this, and the action is one which the mouths of these fishes appear incapable of effecting'.

About the same time Professor J. S. Kingsley, another authority on fishes, was equally categorical.

> One of the species has been generally credited with the faculty of shooting drops of water at insects on low-hanging branches and thus

securing them for food. There does not appear to be any adaptation in the organisation of the mouth for such a feat, and scepticism must be exercised in the acceptance of the statement made. Certainly no recent confirmation of the old story has been given, and the tradition has probably resulted from some misunderstanding.

It is quite clear that during all this time no competent zoologist attempted a first hand investigation. Each authority was content to accept the denials of his predecessors.

Frogs and toads use an entirely different kind of projectile. They catch their insect prey by throwing their tongues at it! The tongue of a land animal is normally fixed at the back of the mouth, leaving the front end free and mobile. Frogs and toads, however, have their tongues fixed at the front edge of the lower jaw, the free end lying backwards along the floor of the mouth. The upper surface is rough with numerous papillae, and moistened with sticky mucus.

The technique used in feeding is for the frog or toad to lie completely still close to some vegetation on which a fly or some other insect may be expected to settle. The mouth must be kept tightly closed, because only when its mouth is closed is it able to breathe. The eyes, however, are large and extremely efficient, capable of detecting the slightest movement in the vicinity.

If you are watching a hunting frog or toad and an insect settles in front of it and within its reach, all you will be conscious of is a kind of click, after which the insect will be seen to have disappeared and the contented amphibian will be making swallowing movements. Exactly what happens when the insect is caught has been analysed by using a high-speed ciné-camera adjusted to take three hundred frames per second.

As soon as the large eyes of the amphibian detect the insect the mouth is opened, the tongue is thrown forward from the back of the mouth and stretched to something like twice its normal length so that the sticky upper surface, now facing downwards, lands on top of the prey, which sticks to it and is conveyed very rapidly back to the mouth. The whole action takes less than one-fifteenth of a second.

In modern times man has made increasing use of animals in his fight against his own enemies, introducing animals into countries where they do not normally occur so that they may use their weapons to control pests attacking his crops.

One of his most successful allies has been the giant neotropical toad, *Bufo marinus*, one of the largest toads in the world, which grows to a length of about nine inches and will comfortably fill a large soup plate. Its appetite is prodigious, and if food is plentiful it will go on eating until its whole body is distended. Besides insects of all kinds it will also eat worms, spiders, centipedes, millipedes, snails and slugs – in fact almost anything of the right size that moves. It has even been known to seize an animal much too large to swallow, releasing it only after a long futile struggle to eat it.

As a pest destroyer it has another great advantage. During the day it lies quiet, coming out to feed at sundown. This is the time when many insect pests also come out of hiding to feed, so escaping the insect-eating birds which are abroad only during the day-time.

Originally *Bufo marinus* was confined to the tropical regions of America from the extreme south of Texas to the northern parts of Argentina. Details of the first transportation from the mainland are not recorded, but we do know that some time in the early part of the nineteenth century some were collected in French Guiana and released in the island of Martinique. Here they flourished and soon became quite common.

From Martinique small consignments were occasionally taken to other islands, until by the middle of the century practically every island in the West Indies could boast its own population of neotropical toads. In all of these islands the animals flourished, and their introduction was followed by considerable decreases in many of the insect pests affecting sugar cane and other crops.

Not all of these introductions, however, were designed to control insect pests. Philip Henry Gosse, the British naturalist who spent some time in Jamaica studying the bird life in the 1840s, has recorded that the toads were first introduced into this island in 1844 to destroy rats which were then abundant. These specimens came from Barbados, where they had achieved a reputation as slayers of young rats. Nowadays this reputation has worn rather thin, and it is doubtful whether any toad will go out of its way to find rats, though it would probably have a go at any young one that passed by.

The remaining chapters in the neotropical toad story are modern, and fantastic. During the years following World War I the Hawaiian sugar planters were suffering increasing losses from the ravages of insect pests. All kinds of remedies were tried with little success. By the 1930s the whole industry seemed faced with ruin.

It was then that Mr C. E. Pemberton, one of the scientists on the staff of the Hawaiian Sugar Planters' Association, got on to the neotropical toad story. On the face of it, it seemed unlikely that a toad could prove of much use where all the resources of modern science had failed. But it was worth a trial, and Mr Pemberton was quite impressed by reports of its success against the white grub pest of sugar cane in Puerto Rico.

Accordingly he went to Puerto Rico. There he collected 148 adult toads, put them in his suitcase and flew back to Honolulu with them as quickly as he could. They were released in two areas of the island of Oahu, and their progress was anxiously watched. The fate of any animal introduced into a new country is always problematical. Fortunately for the sugar planters the neotropical toad was a phenomenal success.

In just over two years it not only became abundant over large areas of Oahu, but more than 100,000 descendants of the original 148 were distributed throughout the other islands of the Hawaiian group. As destroyers of insects the toads exceeded all expectations. As their numbers grew in any area, so the insect pests were reduced to manageable proportions, and the Hawaiian sugar industry was saved.

The fame of the toad spread rapidly across the Pacific, and from all the island groups came requests for consignments. Fortunately neotropical toads breed and grow rapidly. Spawning takes place throughout the year in subtropical regions, each female laying anything up to 10,000 eggs. Tadpoles hatch in two to four days, and in a further three to four weeks the tadpoles have changed to tiny toads a quarter of an inch in length. So there were soon plenty for all.

Distribution was easy. Batches of young toads were put into strong containers with plenty of damp moss, and sent to their new homes by mail. Within ten years of the arrival in Honolulu of the 148 pioneers the Pacific toad population numbered many millions. The toads were by this time firmly established not only throughout the Hawaiian islands but also in the Fijis, the Philippines, Formosa, Australia and New Guinea.

From everywhere came similar reports of successful control of sugarcane pests, and indeed of other insect pests as well. In New Guinea the arch enemy had been a cutworm, whose uncontrollable ravages had made it almost impossible to grow crops of sweet potatoes without recourse to constant dusting with costly insecticides and hand picking of larvae. The arrival of the toads was soon followed by bumper crops of sweet potatoes and the virtual defeat of the cutworm.

Beautifully designed and wonderfully efficient though the tongues of frogs and toads might appear, they seem but primitive prototypes when compared with the tongue of a typical chamaeleon. The chamaeleon is

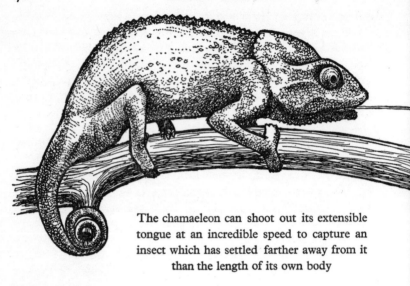

The chamaeleon can shoot out its extensible
tongue at an incredible speed to capture an
insect which has settled farther away from it
than the length of its own body

of course a reptile, common in many parts of Africa and Madagascar,
whose best-known feature is its ability to change its colour to blend with
its surroundings. It is an entirely arboreal creature, spending all its days
in trees and bushes, and preferring to be as far away from the ground
as possible. Few, if any, vertebrate animals indulge in less movement
than the chamaeleon. Indeed it is one of nature's champion sitters. For
hour after hour it will sit completely motionless on a branch, firmly
attached by its feet, which are specially modified for grasping, three
toes on each foot grasping one side of the branch while the other two
grasp the other side. When it does decide to change its position its
movements are so slow that it might well be in great pain, or showing
the immobilising effects of extreme old age.

Despite its sluggish nature, however, it finds no difficulty in obtaining
enough insects to keep itself well fed. To detect its prey it is provided
with two extremely efficient and unusual eyes, each of which is housed
in a very mobile conical turret. And the really strange thing about these
eyes is that they move quite independently of each other, so that while
one is scanning the leaves and twigs above its head the other may be
gazing straight in front, out to the side or even downwards. They are so
mobile, too, that the chamaeleon can look in every possible direction
without having to move its head at all.

With these mobile eyes the chamaeleon becomes instantly aware of

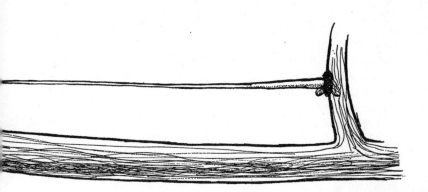

any fly or other insect which comes to rest within its range. Instantly it swivels its eye turrets so that both eyes are focused on the insect. Unless it is more or less directly in front, the chamaeleon will shift the position of its body so slowly that movement is barely perceptible, until it is facing the potential victim. Then, again extremely slowly so that the insect is not alerted, the mouth opens slightly, giving the impression that the chamaeleon is yawning, and from the front of the mouth a globular pink tongue is protruded.

What follows is infinitely more remarkable than the chain of events which occur when a frog or toad snaps up its prey. However carefully the hunting chamaeleon is watched, all that appears to happen is that the tongue is suddenly withdrawn and the jaws snap shut, as though the chamaeleon had decided that the insect was too far away to be captured. Yet the insect has unaccountably vanished, and the observer is certain that it did not fly away, because he was also keeping it in his field of vision. And the chamaeleon is actively chewing and swallowing, while its amazing eyes are already scanning the environment independently looking for further victims.

For a long time naturalists have been fascinated by the incredible speed with which the chamaeleon captures its prey. Only the invention of the high-speed camera made it possible to follow the process in detail. The tongue itself is a complicated structure, as one might expect. It consists of the globular tip, covered with sticky mucus, and a hollow stalk which is extremely elastic and extensible. The tip is 'fired' at the prey by sudden muscular contraction, which shoots it out of the mouth by a mechanism similar to that by which a moist orange or lemon pip can be projected from between the thumb and forefinger by sudden pressure. So elastic is the hollow stalk that a chamaeleon with an average body length of seven inches can capture insects which come to rest up to twelve inches from its nose.

Complete analysis of the movement shows four distinct phases. First the insect is detected by one of the eyes, the other at once swivelling round to face it also. The immediate response is for the mouth to be opened slowly and the tongue brought to the front of the mouth in readiness for firing, while the eyes calculate the range. In the third stage the muscles contract to the required extent to project the tongue just far enough for its sticky tip to pick up the insect. If the tongue were to be projected too far or not far enough the prey would be missed and would escape. In the last phase the greatly extended tongue stalk contracts to return both tongue and prey to the mouth, which closes instantly upon them. The whole firing procedure takes only a fraction of a second, which explains why it cannot be followed by the naked eye however carefully it may be watched.

Such a tongue would be a marvel in any animal, but the astonishing thing about what has been described as the most incredible tongue in nature is that it should belong to one of the slowest moving creatures in the whole animal kingdom.

All spiders use the same method of killing their prey – with poison injected by their powerful jaws. But between them they use a variety of methods of capturing their victims. The best known is by constructing the familiar and beautiful orb web, but the most remarkable is that adopted by a group of spiders commonly known as the bolas or lasso spiders, which are in fact quite closely related to the orb spinners. They are a widely distributed group, having representatives in America, Australia, and Africa.

The traditional weapon used by the South American Indians to capture large animals is the bolas, which consists of one or more fairly large round stones tied to one end of a rope made of plaited hide. It is used in a manner similar to the lasso, being twirled round the head and then released towards the victim. The stone causes the rope to wind itself round the animal, thus bringing it to the ground. The methods used by the bolas spiders to capture their prey are somewhat similar.

An American species of the genus *Mastophora* is widely distributed throughout most parts of the United States, but on account of its nocturnal habits it is not at all well known. It is a rather fat spider of average size which generally lives towards the ends of small branches or twigs several feet above the ground. During daylight the bolas spider remains as immobile as a chamaeleon, lying with its body held close to its perch, thus making it difficult to find. If picked off the perch the spider betrays little sign of being alive. If can be rolled around in the cupped hand without its moving so much as a limb. Even if accidentally dropped to the ground it will still show no evidence of activity. If it is then replaced on its perch it can be found hours later in exactly the same position. This extreme inactivity during the daytime probably serves to protect it from its potential enemies.

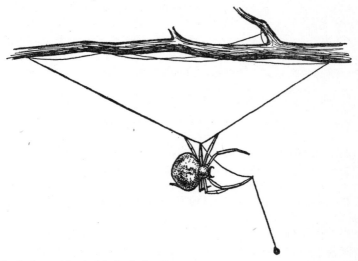

The bolas spider holds its bolas line ready to swing it at an approaching moth or other flying insect

As soon as night has fallen, however, *Mastophora* becomes highly active. Touching the under surface of the twig with its spinnerets it forms a base for a thread. It then crawls several inches along the twig, drawing a thread after it, which it then fixes to a second base. The resulting trapeze-line hangs quite loosely, so that when the spider is suspended in the centre it is well below the twig, thus giving it plenty of space for its subsequent manoeuvres.

From the centre of the trapeze-line the spider now draws out a second line, attaching to it as it is drawn out droplets of viscid silk. Using its hind legs it now combs these droplets downwards until they form a single large globule at the end of the line. This second line is the bolas line with which the spider will catch its night's quota of prey.

Nightfall is also the signal for moths and other nocturnal insects to take to the wing, and it is from these that the bolas spider obtains its food. Poised in the middle of its trapeze-line the spider holds the bolas-line with one of its exceptionally long front legs and waits. In some way it seems to know when a moth is approaching, for it adjusts its position so that at just the right moment it is able to swing the line towards the moth, the sticky globule at the end making contact with the moth's under surface. The victim is brought to an abrupt halt, and its struggles to escape are soon ended as the spider rapidly descends the bolas-line to despatch it with a poison bite from its jaws.

The captured prey is first wound in silk, then its body juices are sucked out at leisure. One moth represents a large meal, and will probably be sufficient to keep the spider going until the following night. When at last the meal is finished the spider cuts the trapeze-line so that the dried remnants of its prey can fall to the ground. Later in the night it may decide that it has had insufficient to eat, in which case it will renew its activities until it has caught a second insect.

Of course the spider will not always make a catch quickly. It may be a long time before a victim comes within range. If nothing has been caught in the first half an hour or so the spider winds in the line and globule and eats them. It then proceeds immediately to make a fresh bolas-line complete with a new globule. Presumably the reason for this renewal, a procedure which will be repeated regularly until success is finally achieved, is that the sticky globule gradually becomes dried up and ineffective.

The eyes of *Mastophora* are very poorly developed, so it is unlikely that sight is the sense used to detect the approaching insect. The most likely explanation of the undoubted fact that the spider can detect it is that the vibrations of the insect's wings are picked up by the suspended thread, and that the spider responds to these vibrations.

Results of careful observations by a number of naturalists suggest that the approach of a moth may not be just a matter of chance, but that it may in fact be attracted in some way towards the bolas thread. On many occasions a moth which had been missed by the bolas globule has been seen to turn round and fly towards it again, sometimes repeating this process several times until it was finally caught. It seems likely that the spider produces some olfactory stimulus which attracts the moths. We do know that moths are susceptible to olfactory stimuli, and that females can attract males from great distances by such means.

The Australian and African bolas spiders both produce similar trapeze-lines and bolas threads complete with sticky globules, but their actual methods of using these threads differ somewhat from that of *Mastophora*. The activities of *Mastophora* were first described in 1903 by Charles E. Hutchinson in the *Scientific American*. Not until 1922 were the similar activities of the Australian *Dicrostichus magnificus* described, when an account was published by Heber A. Longman, who at the time knew nothing of the existence or habits of the American spiders. Part of his account is worth quoting because it shows proximity of behaviour between the two groups of spiders separated by the great width of the Pacific Ocean.

> From its slender bridge it would spin a filament, usually about one and a half inches in length, which was suspended downward: on the end of this was a globule of very viscid matter, a little larger than the head of an ordinary pin, occasionally with several smaller globules above. This filament was held out by one of the front legs, the miniature apparatus bearing a quaint resemblance to a fisherman's rod and line. On the approach of a moth, the spider whirls the filament and globule with surprising speed, and this is undoubtedly the way in which it secures its prey. The moths are unquestionably attracted to an effective extent by the spider, whether by scent or by its colour we cannot say. We certainly could not distinguish the slightest odour. . . . The spectacle of the moth fluttering up to the spider, sometimes two or even three times before it was caught, is one of the most interesting little processes which the writer has ever witnessed in natural history.

The African species, *Cladomelea*, also whirls the globule round and round, but does not wait until suitable prey is in the vicinity. As soon as the bolas-line is formed it is whirled continuously in a horizontal circle for about fifteen minutes. If no insect has been caught in this time the line and the droplet are hauled in and swallowed. After a few minutes' rest the spider proceeds to construct another line, with which it will go on fishing for another fifteen minutes. The process is repeated as many times as necessary until finally an insect is caught. Whereas *Mastophora* and *Dicrostichus* hold the line in one of their long front legs, *Cladomelea* uses one of its short third pair of legs.

CHAPTER 7

Lures and Traps

THE European angler fish, *Lophius piscatorius*, is an extremely grotesque and repulsive-looking creature. It has an enormous flattened head and a great gaping mouth. The small body tapers rapidly to a tiny tail. Fins and tail would be hard put to it to propel the fish through the water at anything more than a snail's pace. But they do not have to, for the angler is a sluggish fish, spending its life just lying on the sea-bed waiting for food to come to it.

Despite this, it makes a good living with the minimum of effort, for it is a fisher of fishes. Its dorsal fin is unusual in that the first few fin rays are well developed and not joined together by skin as fin rays normally are. The first ray is modified to form a remarkable fishing-rod complete with bait. This ray has in fact migrated to the front edge of the upper lip, its base resting on a ball joint. Its extremity is furnished with a fleshy knob, which can be moved around in all directions just in front of the capacious mouth. This knob is the bait which attracts other fish to it.

When angling, *Lophius* lies quite still on the sea-bed with its mouth wide open, the only movement being that of the bait, which is kept constantly on the move. If a curious fish approaches, the angler waits until it is just about to snap at the bait, when there is a sudden upheaval and the unsuspecting fish disappears into the angler's mouth at an incredible speed, the jaws closing behind it. What has actually happened is that at the crucial moment the angler has swallowed violently, drawing in a great volume of water, and the victim has been drawn in with it and swallowed whole. The mouth is specially modified for this method of taking prey. The gill slits have become reduced to two small apertures on either side of the mouth, which ensures that most of the water sucked in goes straight down to the stomach.

Specimens of *Lophius* may grow to a length of up to five feet, half of which is accounted for by the mouth, and very large prey can be swallowed by these individuals. If they are caught in the fishermen's trawl they are of no use as food, but the pancreas is useful because it can yield considerable quantities of insulin.

Lophius piscatorius is only one member of a large group of angler fish which are widely distributed in the seas and oceans of the world. A closely related species, *Lophius americanus*, is found off the eastern coast of North America.

Smaller species are common in tropical waters, the lure varying greatly in form, although always used for the same purpose. Dr William Beebe, the famous underwater explorer, described the reddish frogfish, *Antennarius seaber*, which he captured in the waters around the West Indies.

Its lure was, in size, shape, colour and movement, a perfect imitation of a wriggling, greyish-white worm. While still on board the Antares it devoured three fish. Twice I watched the process, and both times while the prospective prey was at least two inches away, the frogfish opened its mouth and with no apparent effort, created such a maelstrom, such an irresistible current, that the human eye could not see the fish disappear. It simply vanished from sight, the lure was tucked away and we imagined a gleam of satisfaction in the fishy eye.

Phrynelox also has a lure resembling a worm, this time pink in colour, which can coil and uncoil just as a worm on a hook would do. In some cases it seems clear that the lure is designed to catch particular types of fish. *Phrynelox* and *Antennarius*, for example, may be expected to attract fish which normally feed on worms. Another species, the bat-fish *Ogocephalus*, feeds on small crustaceans which live on the sea-bed, and its lure projects downwards. The angling fin ray grows out from the forehead between the eyes and is protected above by a bony extension from the top of the skull.

Angler fish are often heavily disguised with outgrowths which make them look as though they are heavily encrusted with seaweeds and other sedentary marine life. *Phrynelox*, for example, is covered with feathery outgrowths from the skin, which give it an extremely hoary appearance. Presumably these disguises make them less easy to detect by their potential prey.

The most bizarre members of the group are the deep-sea anglers, which live far below the depth to which daylight can penetrate. Unlike *Lophius* and the other shallow-water species, they do not usually live on the ocean bed, which may be at least three miles below the surface. The lure is luminous, otherwise it could not be detected by the potential victims. The light is not produced by the fish themselves, but by bacteria which live within the bait. This is one of the most remarkable examples of symbiosis, in which one organism lives within the body of another for the mutual benefit of both. In this case the fish benefits because the bacteria illuminate its bait and make it of value, while the bacteria gain protection. Not much is really known about these deep-sea anglers, but their lures present a great variety. Some are short, while others may be up to three times the length of the fish, and the terminal knob may be simple and bulbous like that of *Lophius*, or branched and complicated.

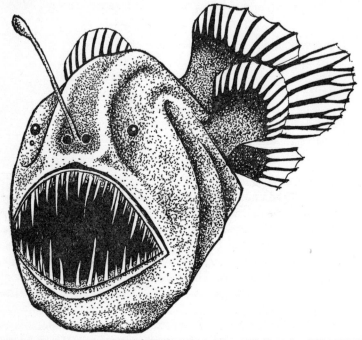

An angler fish has a prominent stalked lure and an enormous mouth armed with a formidable array of sharp teeth

Angler fish are not the only animals to capture their prey by means of lures. The alligator snapping turtle, *Macroclemmys temmincki*, of the eastern and south-eastern regions of the United States also prefers a sedentary life in which it can lure its prey within reach rather than chasing after it. It spends most of its life lying partly buried and completely immobile in the mud on the bed of the river in which it lives. Usually only its head protrudes, with the mouth wide open. The lining of the mouth and the tongue are dark in colour, but on the upper surface of the tongue there is a small worm-like outgrowth covered with red spots which makes it conspicious. This lure can be twitched around to resemble a writhing worm. Fish which swim into the vicinity are attracted to this lure, and as they approach it they come well within the mouth of the turtle, which snaps its jaws closed in a flash and the fish is captured. As with those angler fish provided with a lure which looks like a worm, the alligator snapping turtle captures only fish which normally feed on worms.

The young of quite a number of species of snakes including copperheads, water moccasins and the fer-de-lance use their tails as lures to attract unsuspecting frogs, toads and lizards. These tails are coloured bright yellow, and when the snakes are hungry they are held aloft and waved about. While the potential victims are trying to swallow the bait they fail to notice that the head of the snake has been turned round to face and capture them. After a capture has been made the tail is lowered. Only when the snake again becomes hungry is the lure once more brought into use.

The production of light by the female glowworm in order to attract night-flying males is a well-known phenomenon, but a New Zealand insect uses light to lure its prey. The Waitomo Caves, about two hundred miles north of Wellington, are world famous as the home of one of the great wonders of animal life.

Like most limestone caves, the Waitomo Caves consist of a series of interconnected caverns with a subterranean river running through them. In some of these caverns live the creatures which put on the incredible and unique spectacle to which the caves owe their reputation. In order to witness the phenomenon it is necessary to enter one of the caverns in complete silence and in darkness. The reward is a breath-taking spectacle. The whole roof of the lofty cavern is decorated with myriads of tiny bluish-green lights, producing between them sufficient illumination to reveal the rugged outlines of the cave roof. If someone speaks the lights near the speaker are shut off instantly, the area affected depending upon the loudness of the voice.

The caves are usually known as the 'Waitomo glowworm caves'. Glowworms and fireflies, however, are beetles, but the creature which produces the lights of Waitomo is a mosquito-type fly, *Arachnocampa luminosa*, about twice the size of the common mosquito, and occurring only in New Zealand, where most of the population lives in the Waitomo Caves. Elsewhere they are found only in small numbers and are incapable of providing a real display.

Close investigation of the roof of the Waitomo caves reveals immense numbers of insect larvae fixed to the roof, each within a silken sheath about two inches long, the larva which lives inside the sheath being less than half this length. Its skin is transparent so that all its internal organs

The luminous Waitomo cave gnat larva is fixed to the cave roof, and from
its transparent protective sheath a number of threads furnished with
sticky droplets are suspended

are visible, and its body is grey in colour and without legs. On the underside of the tail is a light-producing organ, the light deriving from
chemical action and not, like the light in the luminous lures of deep-sea
angler fish, from symbiotic bacteria.

From the sheath the larva suspends as many as twenty mucous
threads varying in length from six inches to two feet, each thread dotted
with sticky globules of mucus at intervals of about an inch. The light
shining down from the light-producing organ illuminates these globules
so that each thread looks something like a diamond necklace or a string
of pearls under roof lighting in a jeweller's window.

Other dwellers in the caves are various flies and midges, and the
purpose of the illuminated sticky curtains suspended beneath each larva
is to attract these insects to the roof of the cave and trap them. Struggle
as they will, the trapped insects are firmly caught. The larvae haul in
any line which has secured a victim, eating the line along with the catch.
The lights are switched off when anyone speaks because the suspended
lines also act, as it were, as the ears of the larvae, picking up sound
waves which are taken as warnings of possible danger.

The larval stage of *Arachnocampa* lasts for several months, during which it grows fat and lays down a store of food for subsequent pupation. This results in the formation of a chrysalis which hangs down from the larval sheath suspended by a single thread. Some time later the delicate adult fly emerges. Little is known about this stage as it is seldom seen. It probably lives for only a short time, and so far as is known it does not eat. After mating, the females fly upwards to the roof where they deposit the next generation of eggs. Although any other flying insects brushing against the suspended lines are firmly trapped, by some means not yet understood the adults can brush against the larval traps without any danger of being caught.

The best known and the most widespread of all animal traps is the beautiful orb web constructed by the members of one family of spiders, the Argyopidae. This is in fact the most highly specialised of all the families of spiders. Orb webs are most in evidence in the late summer and autumn, when the early morning dew makes them so conspicuous.

The orb web is one of the most remarkable objects produced by any animal, and its construction is a wonderful example of instinctive

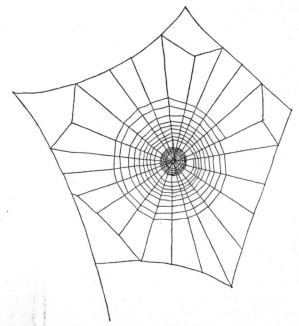

The beautiful orb web produced by the orb spinners. It is either drastically repaired or completely reconstructed every day

activity. But before we examine the steps by which it is produced we must look at it as a completed structure. The whole web is suspended from a horizontal bridge thread which carries virtually the whole weight of the web. The remainder of the framework consists either of two frame threads forming the other two sides of a triangle, or two vertical frame threads descending roughly vertically from either end of the bridge thread. There may or may not be a fourth frame thread running horizontally from the lower ends of these vertical threads to form the lower boundary of the web.

The centre of most orb webs consists of a circular space bounded by a single thread. This is the hub of the web, and from the surrounding thread radii run out in all directions. Some of these terminate at the frame threads while others join section threads which cut off the corners of the framework. Immediately outside the hub is a strengthening zone consisting of a spiral thread which usually runs for three to five turns.

All of the threads so far enumerated consist of dry silk, and form the scaffolding for the really functional part of the web, the trapping zone, without which it would be incapable of capturing prey. This trapping zone consists of a spiral thread of a varying and often large number of turns constructed of a special type of sticky thread, the stickiness being due to minute droplets of a liquid produced by a special gland and fixed at frequent intervals along the whole length of the thread. The inward limit of this viscid thread is some distance away from the outward limit of the hub strengthening zone, leaving between the two spirals a so-called free zone crossed only by the radii.

In addition to the web proper most orb spinners construct a nearby retreat or hiding place. Communication between the spider and its web, by which it will be able to detect the capture of a victim on the viscid spiral, is maintained by a signal thread which runs from the retreat to the hub.

Despite its complexity the orb web is constructed in a remarkably short time, usually less than an hour and in some cases in little more than half this time. It is, too, only a temporary structure, twenty-four hours of use usually causing sufficient damage to necessitate extensive repairs or a complete rebuilding, so that web construction is really a daily chore.

It remains now to examine the steps in the construction of the web. The first event is the fixing of the bridge thread, upon the success of which the whole of the rest of the construction depends. There are in fact several ways in which this is achieved by different species. One common method is similar to that by which baby spiders launch themselves by producing gossamer threads. Having chosen an anchorage for the bridge thread, the spider raises its abdomen into the air and releases a gossamer thread. Carried by what breeze there may be, this thread eventually anchors itself to some distant object, which will then become the other end of the bridge thread.

The spider now proceeds to walk along the gossamer thread in order to replace it by a much stronger thread capable of carrying all the responsibility of a bridge thread. It does not merely strengthen the original thread by adding a stronger thread to it. Instead it picks up the gossamer thread with its forelegs and rolls it up as it proceeds, replacing it by a much stronger new thread which it plays out from its spinnerets.

In another method the spider drops down on two threads which it spins as it is falling. One of these is a thick thread and the other a gossamer thread. This thin thread is then detached, when it will most likely float upwards and anchor itself to some object. In this way the basis of a bridge thread is formed.

By whatever method it is established, the formation of the bridge thread is followed by the completion of the framework and the construction of the radii, and this is succeeded in turn by the construction of the strengthening zone of the hub. The web is now complete except for the viscous spiral. Its construction is not, however, the next step.

What follows is perhaps the most unusual step in the whole construction of the web. Beginning from somewhere outside the hub the spider constructs a spiral of dry silk, working outwards. This forms the temporary scaffolding for the final viscid spiral. Up to now the spider has worked fast, but from now on its movements become much slower and more deliberate. Beginning at the outside of this temporary spiral it proceeds to work inwards, connecting each pair of radii as it goes with a viscid thread. As each connection with a radius is made, one of the hind legs stretches the last section of the spiral rapidly, and this causes the previous uniform sticky coating of the spiral to break up into the characteristic series of viscid drops. The turns of this viscid spiral are more numerous and run closer together than those of the scaffold spiral. As this trapping spiral zone is laid down, so the preceding scaffolding spiral is rolled up by the spider and eaten.

When a victim is caught by the viscid spiral the spider invests it in a shroud of silk after killing it with a bite from its poison jaws. The saliva which is injected is not only poisonous: it also contains protein digesting enzymes which reduce the fleshy contents of the victim to fluid products of digestion, which can then be sucked through the mouth into the stomach, where digestion can be completed. After prey is captured there is some delay while this process of preliminary digestion can be completed before the spider begins its meal.

In contrast to the method used by the orb spinners to capture their prey, the trap-door spiders spin no web at all. They belong to the same group as the large bird-eating spiders. During the daytime they remain in burrows which have hinged lids so well camouflaged that they are virtually impossible to detect. At night, however, these lids are raised, and the occupants lurk at the burrow entrance on the alert for any unsuspecing insect which wanders into the vicinity. Like lightning the prey is seized and killed with an injection from the poisonous jaws, then dragged quickly back into the burrow, the trap-door being securely fixed at the entrance.

As an adaptation to its burrowing habits the trap-door spider is provided with comb-like rakes of short, strong spines along the margins of its jaws. In the construction of a burrow these rakes are used to dig out the earth, the particles of which are then bound together by silk from the spinnerets so that they can be deposited some distance away in parcels of convenient size. As the burrow is excavated its vertical walls are lined with a mixture of saliva and earth to make them waterproof, and then covered with a layer of silk.

Different species use different designs for the construction of their burrow lids. The most effective lid is made up of alternate layers of soil and silk, and is bevelled so as to fit exactly into a correspondingly bevelled opening to the top of the burrow, like a cork in the top of a bottle. This type of lid is heavy enough to close under its own weight. It can be held securely down by the spider from inside its burrow, gripping the underside of the lid with its fangs and front legs while its hind legs maintain a grip on the sides of the burrow.

Other species construct what is known as a "wafer" door consisting of nothing but silk and fitting only loosely into the top of the burrow. Such a door is of course much more easily forced by the spiders' enemies than the more solid door. It can in fact be bitten through if it cannot be raised while held down by the spider.

Although the burrow of a trap-door spider is primarily a special kind of trap for the capture of prey, it is also a defence retreat. Some species show special adaptations to protect themselves from their own enemies. Principal among these is a group of spider-hunting wasps belonging to the family *Pompilidae*. These wasps do not themselves feed upon the spiders; they paralyse them by stinging and then lay a single egg upon each one. The larva which eventually hatches feeds upon the spider. Even the strongest spider is not able to prevent a large pompilid wasp from raising the lid of its burrow once it has located it, and the wasps seem to have considerable ability to detect a burrow however well it may be camouflaged.

Some of the species which produce wafer doors, which would be easily penetrated by these wasps, construct a second line of defence, a secret side chamber leading off horizontally from the lower part of the burrow, and itself closed by a second lid. It is thought that this second retreat may often baffle the predator which has penetrated the first line of defence by removing the lid at the mouth of the burrow. In another species the skin on the hind part of the abdomen is thick, smooth and leathery. If it is disturbed it plunges head first to the bottom of its burrow, where its round abdomen fits tightly like a stopper. No enemy can get a grip on the smooth surface which is also too tough for any sting to penetrate.

One of the traditional methods employed by Africans to capture large wild animals is the pitfall, a pit dug in the ground of sufficient depth to prevent the captured animal from escaping and covered over with sticks, leaves and dried grass to disguise its presence. One ingenious insect, the ant-lion, also digs a pitfall to capture its prey. The ant-lions belong to the insect order *Neuroptera*, whose best-known members are the lace-wings, snake-flies and alder-flies, the adults of which are slender, soft-bodied insects with relatively large gauzy wings. They are very weak fliers.

The actual ant-lion is the larva, and for an insect larva it is highly specialised in structure. It has a large flat head provided with a pair of long sickle-shaped mandibles pointing forward, each with three teeth along its inner edge. The thorax is small and the abdomen oval in shape.

The excavation of the pitfall is a long and laborious process, but always follows the same precise pattern. Having selected a dry and sandy spot, the insect first marks out a circular furrow about three inches in diameter. Placing itself just inside this circle it uses whichever foreleg is on the side nearer the centre of the circle to shovel sand on to its large flat head. The head is then jerked suddenly upwards and outwards so that the sand is thrown outside the limits of the original circle. Backing slightly it proceeds to gather up and dispose of a second load. As one complete circle is cleared so the ant-lion moves slightly inwards to excavate a second circle, each circle excavated being a little deeper than the one outside it. Periodically it will turn round and move in the opposite direction so that each front leg is used in turn, while the other is given a rest. The pitfall when finally completed is shaped like the mouth of a funnel with the centre about two inches below the general ground level.

The pit-fall is now ready for use. The ant-lion buries itself in the bottom so that only its antennae and the tips of its mandibles are showing, and waits patiently, perhaps for an hour or two, perhaps for a day, or perhaps for many days. Eventually an ant or some other ground-dwelling insect comes to the edge of the pit and falls in. Immediately the ant-lion jumps out of hiding to pounce on its prey, its powerful mandibles injecting a dual-purpose saliva which both kills the prey and digests its soft internal muscles and organs, thus having the same properties as the saliva a spider injects into its victims. Sometimes an agile insect may succeed in dodging the first attack and begin to scale the unstable sandy sides of the pit, but it will seldom manage to escape. As it tries to climb the sandy slope the ant-lion begins to toss sand at it, and this bombardment usually sends it toppling back into the bottom of the trap, where the ant-lion instantly pounces upon it.

It may well happen that when the ant-lion has dug its pit one or two small pebbles remain in the bottom, where they would of course be very much in the way. But to the ant-lion they pose no insuperable problem. How it proceeds to rid itself of such a nuisance was described by H. C. McCook as a result of experiments he made in 1907.

> Three pebbles, all larger and heavier than the ant-lion, were dropped into the centre of a pit, where they would be most inconvenient to the occupant and likely to prompt her to remove them. The ant-lion thrust its head beneath a pebble and tried to toss it from the pit. Having failed in this it tried another mode. It placed the end of its abdomen against and a little beneath a pebble and began to push backward. A little time was taken to adjust the pebble so that its centre of gravity would be against the end of the body. Then the animal began to back up out of the pit. All of the pebbles were thus removed.

Because of the intermittent nature of its food supply the life cycle of the ant-lion takes longer than for most insects. It remains in the larval stage for two or three years until it finally pupates, spinning a cocoon around itself. For a couple of months or so the cocoon remains buried in the sand while inside it the adult fly is being formed. When this emerges it has two pairs of large gossamer wings, but like so many insects whose larval stage lasts for a long time, the adult lives for only a few days, sufficient to give it time to mate and lay its eggs in the sand. These hatch in a short time to produce the next generation of ant-lions.

There is one more interesting feature about the ant-lion. Its intestinal canal is incomplete, so that it is incapable of voiding any excrement. This is really no disadvantage to it because all its digestion is done by the saliva which it injects into its victims. What it finally swallows corresponds to what a more normal animal absorbs through the walls of its intestine after its digestive juices have done their work. All the waste substances which an animal normally takes in with its food are left by the ant-lion in the dry husk of its prey.

CHAPTER 8

Blood-Sucking Devices

ANIMALS in a number of widely separated groups have evolved methods of feeding on other animals' blood, thus saving themselves the necessity of obtaining and digesting other kinds of food. All of these animals may be termed 'parasites', since they obtain their nourishment by stealing from other living creatures.

One of the larger and more important phyla in the animal kingdom is the phylum Annelida, comprising the vast group of segmented worms. The phylum consists of three main groups, the Polychaetes, which are the various marine worms used as bait by sea anglers, the Oligochaetes or earthworms, and the leeches, which form the class Hirudinea. The leeches are an interesting group of annelids which have become adapted in structure and modified in behaviour to a life of external parasitism. They are all free-living creatures, attaching themselves to their particular host species whenever a meal is necessary, sucking in sufficient quantities of blood or body fluids before releasing their hold.

At first sight a leech does not bear much resemblance to an earthworm. It is relatively shorter and its body is flattened, and there are no bristles. There are, however, surface rings which look similar to those of an earthworm, but are not, as with the earthworm, external indications of internal segmentation. The body of the leech is segmented internally, but several of these external rings correspond to each of the true segments. One feature, however, is shared by both groups. An individual leech, like an earthworm, can extend or contract its body to a considerable degree.

The most characteristic external features of any leech are its two suckers, one at each end of the body. The one at the head end is very small and often not easy to see. It surrounds the mouth, and its purpose is to fix the mouth firmly to the host's body while the blood or body fluid are sucked out. The much larger hind sucker serves not only to anchor the leech to its host but also to any suitable support when the animal is not feeding. Different kinds of leeches have two different methods of piercing the skin of their victims. In one group there is a circular proboscis which penetrates the host's body, while in the other group the mouth is armed with three serrated jaws which inflict a Y-shaped wound.

The gut of the leech is voluminous, containing a series of pouches which enable some species, including the so-called medicinal leech, to take in up to three times their own weight of blood at a single meal. Such a meal will last the leech for several weeks or even months. To prevent the blood coagulating the leech's saliva contains an anti-coagulant substance called hirudin, which explains why a wound made by a leech may bleed for a long time before healing even after the leech has relinquished its hold. While it is feeding it is virtually impossible to detach a leech without seriously damaging its body. Only when it is ready will it release its hold.

Between meals leeches are sluggish creatures, holding on to stones or water plants with their hind suckers, in no danger of being swept away even in fast-flowing streams. Their normal method of locomotion using their suckers is slow. First the front sucker is released and the body greatly extended. When a suitable new hold is found it is gripped firmly by the front sucker while the hind sucker is released and brought up close to it. The process is repeated until the leech finally settles in a new position which it deems satisfactory. Some species can also swim freely with rather graceful undulations of their flattened bodies.

In Britain two suborders of the class Hirudinea are represented, the Arhynchobdellae and the Rhynchobdellae. The former contains the larger and better known leeches, in which the main distinguishing feature is the possession of the three serrated jaws already mentioned. The best known species is the horse leech, *Haemopis sanguisuga*, widely distributed all over the country in ponds, ditches and slow-flowing streams, where it lives in the mud on the bottom. Normally its body is about one and a half inches long when relaxed, but it can be extended to about six inches when it moves. Despite its name, its three blunt teeth are not even capable of piercing human skin, let alone the tough hide of a horse. Nevertheless in earlier times it was believed by country folk to be capable of sucking the blood of horses. Indeed nine leeches attached to a single horse were believed to be capable of killing it. The land leeches of tropical and subtropical countries are related to the horse leech. They live in damp and shady situations and can be particularly unpleasant, as they have great ability to attach themselves to man or to any large animal passing through their territory.

The only other British member of the horse leech family is the medicinal leech, *Hirudo medicinalis*, once extremely common and wide-spread, but now virtually extinct except in parts of the New Forest and

D

in one or two other areas. In earlier times it was much used by doctors for blood-letting, one or more leeches being attached to the patient to draw off some of his blood. This was the standard treatment for a variety of different ailments. Indeed a jar of living leeches was perhaps regarded as more important to the doctor in those days than his traditional black bag. *Hirudo* was used for this purpose because it was the only British species capable of piercing human skin and taking up a meal of blood.

Even in the first few decades of the nineteenth century leech collecting for the medical profession was quite a profitable occupation, though by this time leeches were becoming scarce through over-collecting. As supplies began to dwindle the doctors turned their attention to the Continent, from where leeches began to be imported in ever increasing numbers, particularly from France. Some idea of the extent to which leeches were still used in the 1830s can be gained from the fact that in 1832 no fewer than 57½ million were imported into this country from France alone. One reason why the French were able to supply these enormous numbers besides satisfying the needs of their own medical profession was that they went in for large-scale leech farming, a form of intensive rearing which was never attempted here. In general size and appearance *Hirudo* is very similar to the horse leech.

Besides the spiders and scorpions, the subphylum Arachnida also includes the class Acari, the mites and ticks, and many of these make a living by sucking blood. Like all the other arachnids they are provided with four pairs of jointed limbs, but the body is not divided into separate cephalothorax and abdomen; the whole body is ovoid in shape with the relatively small legs placed near the front end.

The best known of all the ticks is the sheep tick, *Ixodes ricinus*, sometimes known on account of its shape as the castor-bean tick. An easy way to collect specimens is to take a dog for a walk through a field of infected sheep, when a few of the ticks are almost certain to be brought out firmly attached to its skin. Sheep ticks have pale oval bodies and brown legs and head. Their size varies considerably depending upon how recently they have fed. Normally the head end is buried in the host's flesh, from which the tick obtains its meals of blood. The mouth parts are modified as penetrating and sucking organs. As with leeches, tick saliva is believed to contain an anticoagulant to prevent the sucked blood from clotting while it is awaiting digestion. Unlike leeches, they do not detach themselves after each meal, but remain permanently attached unless forcibly removed or they are tempted to transfer to some other animal which may pass by. So firmly does a sheep tick attach itself to its host that it can be removed only by tearing its body apart. To obtain it undamaged it is necessary first to anaesthetise it by brushing it with benzene, chloroform or alcohol, which causes it to loosen its hold so that it can be picked undamaged off the host's body.

The sheep tick has quite a complicated life history. Mature females lay their eggs on the ground, and from these hatch larvae possessing six legs. These larvae climb to the top of grass stems, where they wait in the hope that a passing sheep will brush against them. If this does happen each larva attaches itself to one of the sheep's hairs, and passes down it until it reaches the skin, into which it plunges its mouth parts, sucking in its host's blood until gorged.

It now releases its hold and drops back to the ground. As the meal is absorbed, so it moults and becomes a nymph with eight legs. Once more it climbs a grass stem, and again attaches itself to a passing sheep, from which it takes a second large meal, and again detaches itself and drops to the ground to digest the meal and moult. This time a mature tick emerges to repeat the same method of attaching itself to a host. Mating takes place on the host's body, followed by the female detaching itself and dropping to the ground, this time to lay its eggs. The chances of being able to attach itself to a passing sheep at any stage are very slender, and the majority of the waiting larvae, nymphs and mature adults perish on their grass stems. Only a tiny minority succeed in finding a host. It is to compensate for this that enormous numbers of eggs are produced.

Ticks do not confine their attentions to warm-blooded animals. Many of them have adapted to life on reptiles, having overcome the problems of penetrating a skin which is covered with hard scales. When a zoo receives a new consignment of snakes and lizards these must be carefully examined for ticks. Often many will be found to be heavily infested. Snake and lizard ticks are sometimes difficult to detect because many of them have developed a protective colour and pattern, making each individual look remarkably like one of the scales of the reptile host. Detecting and removing them is a long and tedious business. Each part of the reptile's skin has to be carefully checked over and each tick must be brushed with spirit and then extracted with tweezers. Every effort is made to ensure that new arrivals are completely clear of parasites before they are put on exhibition, because an outbreak of ticks in an exhibition cage necessitates removing the inhabitants and thoroughly disinfecting the cage. The infestation, too, may spread to neighbouring cages.

The thick shell of a tortoise would seem to be impenetrable, yet in Malaya a large tick can bore a hole right through the shell of a land tortoise. During the slow drilling it exudes a milky fluid, which may possibly help to soften the hard material. When its mouth parts finally reach a blood vessel beneath the shell they become firmly fixed by a cement-like substance, so that it is impossible to detach the tick from the host. Yet a tick can apparently detach itself at will, because many tortoise shells show old tick wounds.

Many different kinds of insects make a living by sucking the blood of warm-blooded animals, and none of these is better known or more efficient than the mosquito, which belongs to a very large insect order, the Diptera or flies, characterised as the name indicates by the possession of a single pair of wings. Other winged insects always possess two pairs.

The mouth parts of the mosquito have become modified to form a well-nigh perfect two-way hypodermic syringe, capable of both injecting saliva into the flesh of a victim and then sucking some of its blood. The whole apparatus consists of six incredibly sharp stylets lying in a lower lip or labium which is so deeply grooved that the edges almost meet above the stylets. Lying in the middle line on the bottom of this

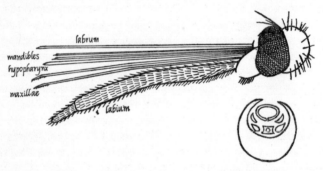

The mouth parts of a mosquito, slightly separated for clarity (above). Below: is a transverse section showing how the six stylets fit into the deeply grooved labium

groove is the hypopharynx, a hollow tube with a minute channel running through the middle of it from the salivary glands to open at its tip. On either side of this hypopharynx lie the two maxillae whose ends are serrated. Above the maxillae lie a pair of mandibles which are needle sharp but unserrated, and between them, completing the six stylets, is an upper lip or labrum, which is deeply grooved underneath. It is through this groove, virtually a closed tube, that the mosquito sucks in the blood of its victims.

All the stylets are rigid structures, but the labrum is soft and fleshy.

When a hungry mosquito lands on the skin a suitable spot is chosen and the six stylets are plunged vertically into it, the labrum being folded back in the form of a loop because it has no penetrative powers. Saliva is then forced down the tube of the hypopharynx, and it is this saliva which is believed to cause the irritation and swelling which usually accompany a mosquito bite. There are so many minute blood vessels beneath the victim's skin that the stylets must have penetrated at least one of these, and the blood is then drawn up through the ventral groove of the labrum.

Incidentally only female mosquitoes are equipped with this piercing mechanism. The mouth parts of males are relatively rudimentary, and are capable of sucking only liquids which are available on a surface. Their antennae, however, are much more feathery than those of the females.

There are two main genera of mosquitoes: *Anopheles* and *Culex*. When resting on a surface the members of the two genera can be easily distinguished. All *Culex* species rest with the body held more or less parallel with the surface, whereas *Anopheles* species always rest with their heads pointing downwards and their abdomens pointing upwards. From the medical point of view *Anopheles* species are the more important, because it is only these which can transmit malaria.

The connection between malaria and the anopheline mosquitoes was finally established as recently as 1897 by Sir Ronald Ross after two and a half years of intensive research. Once he had established that the organisms responsible for malaria were conveyed from infected to healthy men by mosquito bites the battle against malaria was intensified.

Their breeding methods have an important bearing on the methods used to combat mosquitoes in malaria-infested countries. All mosquitoes lay their eggs in water, and these hatch out to form completely aquatic larvae. Again there are significant differences between culicine and anopheline larvae. Anopheline larvae lie horizontally just beneath the surface of the water, taking in respiratory air through a pair of breathing tubes or spiracles on the eighth abdominal segment. In culicine larvae only the tail end comes near to the water surface, air being taken in through long breathing tubes which project upwards from this end of the body. The rest of the body hangs downwards in the water. The open ends of the anopheline spiracles and culicine breathing tubes are both covered with an oily secretion which is water repellent and thus resists blockage. It also helps to keep them at the surface. This has an important bearing on the modern methods used to destroy mosquitoes.

To kill adult mosquitoes in any significant numbers is virtually impossible, but in their larval stages they are much more vulnerable. If oil is spread upon the surface of the water in which the larvae are living this destroys the water-repellent properties of their own oily secretions, and as a result water enters their breathing tubes and they are drowned. A relatively small amount of oil will form a film of adequate thickness over a considerable expanse of water. This treatment of open stretches of water, coupled with large-scale draining of swamps, has gone a long way towards reducing the incidence of malaria in tropical countries where it is endemic.

Midges are closely related to but much smaller than mosquitoes, adults seldom exceeding one-tenth of an inch in length, but their efforts to suck our blood can be every bit as irritating. Only certain species are equipped with apparatus which enables them to suck human and other mammal blood, and as with mosquitoes it is only the females which are so equipped. One species, *Culicoides impunctatus*, is notoriously troublesome in the Highlands of Scotland during the summer months.

Mosquitoes are by no means the only insects to indulge in bloodsucking. Another important group are the fleas, which constitute a separate insect order, the Aphaniptera. All fleas are parasites, and none of them has wings. The mouth parts of the adults are specialised for piercing skin and sucking blood from the mammals and birds on whose bodies they live.

All fleas are extremely flattened from side to side, and covered with a smooth, hard skin, these two features making it easy for them to move quickly through hair or feathers. Their legs are relatively long and well developed, hence the leaps for which they are notorious. The human flea, *Pulex irritans*, may jump a vertical height of more than seven inches, no mean feat for such a tiny insect. For an insect living among the fur or feathers of its host sight is obviously not an important sense, and the flea has lost the typical insect compound eyes, retaining only a single simple eye on each side of the head.

The most important flea from the medical point of view is the oriental rat flea, *Xenopsylla cheopis*, the organism responsible for transmitting the bubonic plague bacillus, *Bacillus pestris*, from rats to man. The bacillus is carried in the gut of the flea, and is thus deposited in its faeces on the skin of its human host. If this occurs in the neighbourhood of a bite from the flea, the bacteria may well be rubbed into the skin by the consequent scratching.

Lice, like fleas, are also parasitic insects. They form the order Anoplura, which contains two distinct sub-orders, the Mallophaga or biting lice, which live almost exclusively on birds and feed on minute particles of skin and feathers, and the Siphunculata or sucking lice, which have a set of piercing and sucking mouth parts similar to the mosquitoes. Sucking lice live only on mammals, and there are very many species, because almost every mammal species has its own exclusive louse. There is even an elephant louse.

Their food consists of the blood of their hosts – more nutritious, one would think, than that of the biting lice – and this is obtained by means of a hypodermic needle formed from the maxillae and the labium. The skin of the host is pierced, saliva is forced in through the wound to prevent coagulation of the blood and this is then sucked up and digested. Lice are less active than fleas and are therefore more easily caught by the expert who wishes to examine them. If a mammal is shot the naturalist who wishes to capture its parasitic fleas must be very much on the alert, for they will leave its body almost immediately. Lice, however, will not begin to leave in search of another host until the body is quite cold.

To us the most important of all the lice is the human louse, *Pediculus humanus*. Because it can carry and transmit the micro-organisms of some of our most dreaded diseases, it is one of the great scourges of humanity. Two races are recognised, the head louse, *Pediculus humanus capitis*, and the body louse, *Pediculus humanus corporis*. Although the body louse has been largely eradicated in civilised communities, the head louse still appears even in Britain today where people live under unhygienic conditions. It is now much more common in children than in adults, and among the children girls are infected more than boys.

The most important diseases transmitted by body lice are typhus, trench fever and relapsing fever, all of which are readily transmitted from one person to another under crowded and unhygienic conditions. It seems likely that the louse has been responsible for the transmission of more human disease than any other insect. Until Florence Nightingale's revolutionary work in the Crimean War the number of typhus deaths among combatant armies was appalling. Thanks to her work in founding modern standards of hospital nursing in peacetime as well as in wartime, typhus was practically wiped out in civilised countries, only to reappear with renewed vigour with the outbreak of the 1914 war. During the first year of hostilities the little country of Serbia lost no fewer than 150,000 civilians through typhus, introduced by Austro-Hungarian prisoners of war. In Russia some three million people died of the same disease between 1917 and 1920, while the enormous number of soldiers who fell victim to typhus on the Western Front has never been calculated, but would certainly bear comparison with the number killed in the fighting.

Transmission of disease organisms both by lice and by mosquitoes is easy. The organisms are sucked up with the host's blood, and then passed to the next host along with the saliva which is injected into its blood before the insect sucks in its meal.

Among the most repulsive of the blood-sucking insects of man are the bed-bugs. These are members of the order Hemiptera, a very large group which also includes the comparatively innocuous and numerous aphids, mealy-bugs, scale-insects, white-flies, shield-bugs, capsid-bugs, frog-hoppers and leaf-hoppers.

The bed-bug, *Cimex lectularius*, is without wings, but its mouth parts are modified to form an efficient blood-sucking apparatus, consisting of a sharp compound stylet formed from the modified mandibles and maxillae sheathed within the grooved lower lip or labium. It is a nocturnal animal, hiding by day in crevices in woodwork or behind torn wallpaper. At night it comes out of hiding and has an uncanny ability to seek out and steal a meal from anyone unfortunate enough to be sleeping in the room. Not least of its disadvantages is the particularly vile smell which accompanies it. It is said that if the legs of a bed are placed in bowls of water to prevent the bug from climbing up them, it will ascend the walls and crawl along the ceiling until it is above the sleeper and then drop down upon him.

Typically it is an inhabitant of rather warm climates, but it has been in Britain for a long time, quite probably brought here by the Romans. The first recorded reference to this particularly unsavoury pest is an account of an apparently successful attempt by a Dr Penny in 1583 to disinfest a house, recorded in Moffet's *Theatrum Insectorum*. He was summoned urgently to

a little village called Mortlake near the Thames, to visit two noble ladies, who were much frightened by perceiving the prints of wall-lice, and were in doubt of I know not what contagion. But when the matter was known, and the wall-lice were catched, he laught them out of all fear. Against those enemies of our rest in the night our merciful God hath furnished us with remedies, that we may fetch out of old and new writers, which being used will either drive them away or kill them. For they are killed with the smoke of Oxe-dung, Horse-hair, Swallows, Scolopendra, Brimstone, Vitriol, Arsenick, Verdi-grease, Lignum aloes, Bdellium Fern, Spatula foetida, Birthwort, Clematis, Myrtils, Cummin, Lupins, Snotgrass, Gith and Cypress. But the best way is with the curtains drawn about the bed, so to shut in the smoke that it can have no vent.

How man acquired the bed-bug as a parasite poses an interesting problem. Most mammals are preyed upon by mosquitoes, lice and fleas, and in many cases each mammal species has its own parasite species, which was evolved along with the mammal. As any species of mammal evolved from the ancestral species, so its parasites evolved from those of the ancestral mammal. But the bed-bug cannot have been evolved in this way because no other primate, the group to which man belongs, is parasitised by any bug. In fact the only other animals to be so parasitised are bats and birds, and the particular species which is parasitic on man on many is more closely related to the bugs which live on bats than to those which live on birds. It seems virtually certain, therefore, that man acquired his bed-bug from the bats which shared the same caves with him during the early stages of his evolution.

Evidence to support this theory was produced in 1965 by Professor Dalibor Povolny, a Czechoslovakian zoologist, who discovered in a cave in Afghanistan a population of bats infested with bugs which seemed to him to be identical with *Cimex lectularius*. Specimens which he collected from this cave were subsequently crossed with genuine bed-bugs belonging to the species *Cimex lectularius* obtained from places as far apart as Cairo and Berkeley, California. The offspring in both cases proved to be completely fertile, and microscopic examination of the cell nuclei showed that the chromosome complement of the cave bugs was in every respect identical with that of the human parasites, thus proving beyond reasonable doubt that the bugs found parasitising the bats did indeed belong to the same species as those infesting man.

Moths and butterflies live by sucking juices such as nectar, perspiration, shed blood, and even the discharge from tear glands. But in 1967 Hans Banziger discovered in Kuala Lumpur a blood-sucking moth, *Calyptra eustrigata*. He had observed that individuals of many related species derived nourishment by wandering over the bodies of cattle and other large mammals, imbibing such liquid discharges as these animals produced. What struck him about *Calyptra eustrigata* was that it seemed to obtain what it wanted from one spot on its host's body. The first specimen he observed was feeding on the body of a tapir, and he took a flash photograph of it, with the result that the tapir got up and bolted away. When the photograph was developed he realised for the first time that this particular moth was different from all other moths which he had observed. The proboscis of the normal butterfly and moth is soft and pliable, and when it is sucking up surface juices the terminal part of the proboscis is bent so as to lie flat on the surface. The proboscis of *Calyptra*, however, was obviously a rigid structure and from the photograph it seemed to be piercing the surface of the tapir's skin.

To investigate further Hans Banziger captured some specimens of the moth and encouraged them to explore his arm. He was soon able to discover from painful experience that the moth's proboscis was rigid and was capable of penetrating skin to a depth of about six millimetres. He was also able to observe some tiny droplets of saliva running down the outside of the proboscis, its function probably being the same as that of the saliva injected by other blood-sucking insects, to prevent the blood from coagulating. So far little more is known about the blood-sucking moth. The most interesting question is whether it acts as a carrier for any disease organisms.

The last group of blood-sucking animals which we have to consider is the vampire bats, around which so much completely false legend has grown up. The true vampire bats are a group of small bats about three and a half inches long and extremely well adapted to their chosen mode of feeding. The upper incisor teeth are long and extremely sharp, and have the remarkable ability to carve a deep groove through the skin of a human being without waking him. From this groove blood flows freely, to be lapped up by the bat until it is satiated. Vampire bats, of which the best known species is *Desmodus rotundus*, are found only in central and the northern parts of South America.

Vampire bats are strong fliers, but unlike most other bats can move freely on the ground. In order to avoid waking a potential victim, the vampire usually lands some little distance away and then scuttles swiftly along the ground towards him. The vampire usually attacks exposed parts of the body such as the toes, fingers, ears, face or neck. It is even credited with fanning its victim's face by beating its wings in order to keep him asleep while it enjoys its meal. Opportunities for feeding may not be particularly frequent, so the vampire bat tends to lap up so much blood that it becomes too heavy to fly, in which case it has to crawl away along the ground, going into hiding until it has digested enough of its meal to become airborne again.

Fiction and films have used the relatively harmless vampire bat to build up a fearsome legend of a blood-sucking monster. Even in medieval times it was believed that the vampire was the restless soul of a dead man, which left the grave on moonlight nights to suck the blood of the living. The only way to destroy the vampire was to exhume the body and drive a stake through its heart. In fact of course the vampire bat is scarcely more harmful than a giant mosquito of similar size would be.

CHAPTER 9

Insect Stings

MODERN classification recognises no fewer than twenty-two different insect orders, but in only one of these are true stings developed. This order, the Hymenoptera, contains the saw-flies, wood-wasps, gall-wasps, chalcid-wasps, ichneumon flies, true wasps, bees and ants. It has the distinction of including more British species than any other insect order, with a total of nearly 6,200, its nearest rivals being the order Diptera, the flies, with about 5,200 species, and the order Coleoptera or beetles with about 3,700 species.

All female insects have a special organ known as the ovipositor situated towards the end of the abdomen. Its primary function, as its name suggests, is the laying of eggs, but in many of the Hymenoptera it has been modified to form the sting which is such a prominent feature of these insects. The wide variety of uses to which this modified ovipositor is put by different types of Hymenoptera is such a fascinating story that it seems worth giving in full, even though in some of the examples the ovipositor cannot strictly be regarded as a weapon either of attack or defence.

The order is subdivided into two sub-orders, the Symphyta, which consist of the saw-flies and wood-wasps, and the Apocrita, which includes the gall wasps, ichneumon flies, chalcid-wasps, bees, true wasps and ants.

Saw-flies and wood-wasps use their ovipositors to provide protection for their eggs and larvae. They are exclusively plant feeders, and their most distinctive feature is that the ovipositor of the female is modified as a saw, with which she makes slits or pockets on plant leaves or stems, laying one egg in each.

Saw-fly larvae, which are similar in general appearance to those of butterflies and moths, are in the main foliage eaters and as such many of them are serious pests. One of the best known is the gooseberry saw-fly, *Pteronus ribesii*, which eats the leaves of gooseberry and currant bushes. The little yellow-spotted caterpillars can be a nuisance in the garden, but to the commercial fruit grower their attentions can be disastrous. Conifer plantations sometimes suffer from plague attacks of two closely related pine saw-flies, *Diprion pini* and *Diprion sertifer*, whose larvae feed on pine needles. In particularly bad years whole plantations of conifers can be completely stripped of their needles. Immense damage was done to pine plantations in East Anglia through the efforts of these two saw-flies between 1926 and 1929.

Wood-wasps are closely related to the saw-flies, but they are very much larger. The best known species is the giant wood-wasp, *Sirex gigas*, which measures about an inch and a half in length, not including the very long ovipositor, which projects well beyond the end of the abdomen. It is a yellow and black insect and is feared by many people because of its superficial resemblance to the hornet. It is, however, completely harmless, and can be readily distinguished because it lacks the prominent 'waist' characteristic of all true wasps, both solitary and social.

Sirex gigas and the related blue *Sirex cyaneus* lay their eggs in the wood of conifers, never attacking broad-leaved trees. The stout ovipositor is used to bore a hole into the solid wood, and at the bottom of the drill a single egg is laid. The larvae on hatching proceed to bore slowly through the wood, living on the shavings which they scrape off with their powerful jaws. They remain in the wood for two or three years before pupating. However far into the trunk the larva may have penetrated previously, it always comes near to the surface before it pupates, so that when the adult wood-wasp finally emerges it has only about half an inch of wood to negotiate before breaking free.

All the members of the sub-order Apocrita are distinguished from the members of the first sub-order Symphyta because the first abdominal segment is firmly fused with the thorax, and the second abdominal segment is constricted to form the characteristic 'waist'. The larvae, too, are grubs without legs. The sub-order is further subdivided into two groups, the Parasitica, whose larvae are nearly always parasitic, and the Aculeata, in which the ovipositor forms a true poison-injecting sting. The Parasitica group contain three families, the Cynipoidea or gall-wasps, the Chalcidoidea or chalcid-wasps and the Ichneumonoidea or ichneumon flies.

Many different kinds of living organisms cause abnormal growths on plants called galls, but the most important of these gall producers are the gall-wasps. For some quite inexplicable reason the plant most prone to gall formation is the oak tree. As the tree bursts into leaf in the spring so its two best-known galls develop, the oak-apple and the hard marble gall. The oak-apple in England has a special significance as the emblem worn by royalists on Oak-apple Day or Royal Oak Day, celebrated on 29 May, the birthday of Charles II. It commemorates his escape by hiding in an oak tree after he was defeated by Cromwell at the Battle of Worcester in 1651.

If you cut open an oak-apple you will find it contains a number of separate chambers, each occupied by a tiny grub of a particular kind of gall-wasp known as *Biorhiza pallida*. After pupation within the gall the adult wasps emerge, their points of exit being betrayed by neat round holes in the surface of the oak-apple. These adults consist of full-winged males and females which cannot fly, some being completely without wings while others have vestigial but quite functionless wings. After mating, which occurs in July, the flightless females crawl down the trunk of the oak tree and into the soil at its base. There they pierce the small lateral roots of the tree with their ovipositors, laying a single egg at the bottom of each drill. The developing eggs stimulate the formation of small galls on the roots.

By the end of the summer the larvae have grown to full size, pupated, and are ready to emerge. All the adult gall-wasps which emerge from these root galls are wingless females, and there are no males around to fertilise them. Nevertheless they make their way out of the soil and up the trunk of the tree, where they lay unfertilised parthenogenetic eggs in the terminal buds of twigs. In the following spring the eggs hatch out, and by early May the infected buds are already beginning to swell. By the end of the month the oak-apple galls are fully developed.

The much harder spherical marble galls are similarly caused by another species of gall-wasp, *Cynips kollari*. This time, however, each gall contains only one grub. One curious feature of this gall-wasp is that no one has ever found a male. On one occasion a naturalist at the British Museum collected more than 12,000 galls and kept them until the adult insects emerged in the autumn. He was rewarded by more than 12,000 female gall-wasps, but not a single male appeared. Further research will no doubt show whether the marble gall does indeed belong to an entirely female society or whether males do occur somewhere along the line.

Whether saw-flies, wood-wasps and gall-wasps can be said to use their ovipositors as weapons is perhaps a matter of opinion. They certainly do not use them to combat enemies, but on the other hand it can be argued that they are used as protective weapons because they enable the eggs to be laid in positions where enemies cannot readily reach them.

With the ichneumon flies there is no shadow of doubt that their ovipositors are used as offensive weapons. The females lay their eggs either on the surface or actually in the tissues of other insect larvae. As the host larvae grow, their bodies are devoured by the ichneumon larvae which hatch out from the deposited eggs. These finally pupate within the now empty skin of the host. The naturalist who rears batches of caterpillars in the hope of obtaining stocks of a particular butterfly or moth is often rewarded instead with a worthless collection of ichneumon flies, the caterpillars having at some stage in their development been parasitised by ichneumon flies which laid their tiny eggs on or in their bodies.

The story of the ichneumon fly infestations of the caterpillars of the common large white butterfly, *Pieris brassicae*, provides a classic example of the activities of ichneumon flies. One of the most common of our ichneumon flies is *Apanteles glomeratus*, a tiny insect which specialises in laying its eggs in the growing caterpillars of the large white butterfly. It is so small relative to the caterpillar that it can lay upward of one hundred eggs in a single caterpillar, introducing the eggs into the body of its victim with its ovipositor. When the ichneumon eggs hatch the tiny larvae feed upon the fat stores of the host caterpillar, avoiding more vital tissues which would kill it. Eventually the caterpillar reaches the stage when it would normally pupate, but because its food stores have been stolen by the parasites it cannot sustain a long pupation and dies. By this time the tiny parasite larvae are also fully grown and ready to pupate, which they do by spinning tiny yellow cocoons on the surface of the dead host caterpillar. It has been calculated that attacks by *Apanteles* account for some 35 per cent of all large cabbage white caterpillars, so this particular ichneumon fly certainly plays an important part in the control of this butterfly.

Even *Apanteles*, however, does not have things all its own way. An even smaller ichneumon fly, *Hemiteles nannus*, actually lays its eggs on the *Apanteles* larvae which are themselves developing within the body of the butterfly caterpillar. It is apparently able to detect the presence of its own victims despite their being hidden within the body of another animal. *Hemiteles* is described as a secondary parasite, since it parasitises an animal which is already parasitising another. Even this is not the end of the story so far as the internal inhabitants of the cabbage white larvae are concerned, for the secondary parasite *Hemiteles* is in it turn parasitized by the minute chalcid-wasp, which lays its eggs in the bodies of its larvae. The existence of parasite chains, in which each parasite could be itself parasitised by a smaller creature was amply summed up by Jonathan Swift in his well known verse:

> So, naturalists observe, a flea
> Hath smaller fleas that on him prey;
> And these have smaller fleas to bite 'em,
> And so proceed *ad infinitum*.

The final chapter in the complicated story of the parasites of the cabbage white butterfly is concerned with those larvae which escape all attacks and come through to successful pupation. They often fall victim to another small chalcid-wasp, *Pteromalus puparum*, which apparently never lays its eggs on the caterpillars, but waits until the pupae have been formed.

A well-developed sense of smell, which they are known to possess, is believed to be the means by which female ichneumon flies detect their potential victims, no matter where they may be hidden.

Our largest and most spectacular ichneumon fly is *Rhyssa persuasoria*. It has a bluish-black body with white markings on the abdomen and its legs are red. The total length of the body is about one and a quarter inches, but the female has an extraordinarily long ovipositor measuring about one and a half inches. This, however, is no ornament but a vital necessity, for *Rhyssa* preys upon the larvae of the giant wood-wasp *Sirex gigas*, and it must be able to bore into solid wood until its long ovipositor locates one of these larvae. The single egg is then passed down the long tube to be inserted in the larval body.

Observations have shown that a *Rhyssa* female can bore a hole one and a quarter inches deep into solid wood in about twenty minutes. Before undertaking any boring operations the female will explore the surface of a tree-trunk carefully with her antennae, almost certainly seeking out likely places for boring by being able to detect the *Sirex* larvae beneath. Having apparently located one she often seems to become excited, and then commences operations. It sometimes happens that she does not encounter a larva, perhaps because it has recently moved away but has left its scent. In this case she continues her search, repeating her boring operations at the next likely spot. The channel which passes down the centre of her ovipositor is so slender that the egg is squeezed completely out of shape as it passes down but is reshaped as it is deposited on the victim's body.

Rhyssa has played an important part in combating wood-wasp attacks on conifer forests in New Zealand. In 1926 the New Zealand authorities were becoming alarmed by a significant increase in the occurrence of the wood-wasp *Sirex noctilio*. Its larval burrows were beginning to cause widespread damage to the trees. It was decided to import specimens of *Rhyssa persuasoria* and release them in the forests in the hope that they might combat the growing menace of the wood-wasps. By 1936 these importations had been so successful that a New Zealand authority wrote: '*Rhyssa* is certainly the most spectacular beneficial insect which has been introduced into this country'. In Britain *Sirex* is so effectively controlled by *Rhyssa* that almost every *Sirex* larva becomes parasitised, so that only a tiny proportion of all the larvae deposited survive to produce adults.

This seems an appropriate point at which to mention the pioneer work of the Farnham House Laboratory at Farnham Royal in Buckinghamshire in developing methods of biological control with insects. It was opened in 1927 as a branch of the Imperial Institute of Entomology, its function being to collect and breed stocks of insects which were known to be parasites of economically harmful insects. These could then be distributed to any part of the world where these insects existed in pest proportions. The collection of *Rhyssa* larvae and their export to New Zealand was one of the earliest and most successful of the Laboratory's efforts. In the twelve years from its foundation in 1927 until the outbreak of war in 1939 the Farnham laboratories distributed nearly forty million insects to all parts of the world to combat various insect pests, and had achieved many spectacular successes.

Like the ichneumon flies the chalcid-wasps are also exclusively parasitic in their larval stages. There is one important difference between them, however. Chalcid-wasps are very much smaller insects than ichneumon flies, some of them, commonly called fairy flies, measuring not more than one-fiftieth of an inch in length. In consequence they generally lay their eggs within the eggs of their hosts, and not in or on their larvae. Some of the chalcid-wasps which lay their eggs in the eggs of certain moths have evolved an extraordinary method of multiplying. When the moth egg hatches the chalcid egg begins to develop into a mass of cells. Instead of forming themselves into a chalcid larva, however, they proceed to divide themselves into a large number of small groups of cells, each of which gives rise to a separate chalcid larva, which will eventually develop into a full-grown chalcid-wasp after pupation. In this way a single egg can result in the production of dozens of chalcids. One chalcid, *Litomastix*, may produce as many as a thousand adults from a single egg laid inside an egg of the silver-Y moth, *Plusia gamma*. Sometimes the female chalcid lays several eggs, in which case several thousand chalcid-wasps may ultimately be produced from a single moth egg.

Chalcid-wasps have also played an important part in modern biological control of insect pests. A chalcid in fact featured in one of the first successful attempts at biological control. Early in this century a new insect pest appeared in Britain, the greenhouse white fly, *Trialeurodes vaporariorum*. It rapidly established itself as a major enemy of those engaged in food production under glass. The fly was particularly destructive of tomatoes and cucumbers. The white fly had presumably been introduced here from elsewhere, and there is some evidence that it came originally from Brazil. For some years the only effective control of the white fly was fumigation of the greenhouses with hydrogen cyanide, a deadly poisonous gas which, despite the utmost precautions, resulted in a number of deaths. The alternative method of control was discovered quite unexpectedly, when a number of minute chalcid-wasps were observed preying upon the white flies in a greenhouse in Elstree, Hertfordshire, in July 1926.

The chalcid, *Encarsis formosa*, a tiny insect only about one-fortieth of an inch long, was itself unknown in this country before this discovery, and is thought to have been introduced along with a consignment of plants from abroad. Its possible importance was realised at once, and a number were taken to the research station at Cheshunt, Hertfordshire. Here they were reared intensively and by the following summer the value of *Encarsis* in clearing a greenhouse of white fly had already been established beyond doubt. From that time the white fly ceased to be the menace to the market gardener which it had been hitherto.

Another chalcid-wasp, *Aphelinus mali*, proved an equally effective enemy of the woolly aphid in apple orchards in many parts of the world. In Britain, however, it has been less successful. Apparently our climate is too cold for it to flourish.

In the last group of the Hymenoptera, the Aculeata, the ovipositor no longer serves its original purpose. Instead it has become modified to form a sting through which minute amounts of virulent poison can be injected into enemies and victims. The eggs now pass out of the body through a new opening near the base of the sting. Since the sting is a modified ovipositor only females possess it, the males being defenceless.

Bees normally use their stings only in defence, and will not sting unless they are handled roughly. The bee sting consists of a bulb in which the venom is stored, and three long rigid structures enclosing between them the canal which leads from the bulb to the tip. One of these forms a curved sheath partially covering the other two lying below it. These are the lancets, and they are provided with barbs at their extremities. The whole sting is normally carried retracted within a sting chamber.

When a worker or a queen bee has decided to use its sting it is first protruded from the sting chamber and thrust at the potential victim. The tips of all three elements penetrate only a short way, but the two lancets begin sliding backwards and forwards alternately, their barbs ensuring that the whole sting sinks deeper into the flesh. The barbs make it difficult for the bee to withdraw its sting from the soft flesh, so that the whole apparatus is usually torn out of the bee's body when it flies away, after which the bee will not live for long. Curiously enough, when a bee stings one of its own kind it is able to withdraw without causing itself any damage. The sting of the wasp is similar, but the barbs are smaller so that it can be withdrawn without causing any damage to the wasp.

From our point of view, however, the most interesting members of the *Aculeata* are the various species of solitary wasps. Whereas bees feed exclusively on plant products, all wasp larvae are carnivorous, and the solitary wasps have developed the most ingenious methods of providing for their larvae when they hatch out and their parents will not be present to feed them.

Although there is a great diversity of solitary wasps, their modes of life follow a fundamentally similar pattern. Before she lays an egg the female prepares some kind of chamber for its reception, usually a hole in the ground which she has excavated, or more rarely a chamber of earth which she has constructed attached to a plant. She then proceeds to capture a small living creature, which may be an insect, an insect larva or a spider, by stinging it so that it is paralysed, and depositing it in the prepared nest. She then lays a single egg on it, so that when the larva hatches it has a store of food on which it can feed until it is ready to pupate. Sometimes the victim is stung so skilfully that it remains alive, though unable to move, and in other cases the victim dies, but in this case the venom acts as an antiseptic so that it will not decay before the larva is ready to start its feed.

Two genera of British solitary wasps are true wasps, related to the well-known common social wasps. *Eumenes coarctata* is the potter wasp, which makes beautifully designed vase-shaped cells of earth attached to the stem of heathers and other small woody plants. Each cell is stocked with a number of tiny caterpillars, and one egg is suspended from the roof. It seems that while still suspended from the roof the newly-hatched larva feeds on the first caterpillar. This seems to be an insurance against being crushed by the collection of paralysed caterpillars while it is still very small. The various species of *Odynerus* have similar habits, though some species stock their cells with the larvae of beetles instead of the caterpillars of butterflies and moths.

The remainder of our solitary wasps belong to the group of digger wasps, which excavate a burrow in the ground for the reception of their eggs. The main differences between them concern the kind of victims they select for their offspring. *Ammophila* species supply their cells with non-hairy caterpillars, whereas *Pompilus* species always stock theirs with spiders. Flies form the only diet for the larvae of *Crabro* species, and *Cerceris* species always prey upon weevils. *Philanthus* species capture bees, *Gorytes* species specialise in dragging frog-hopper nymphs from their protective covering of cuckoo-spit, while members of the genus *Pemphredon* stock their nests with paralysed aphids.

Because of their particularly effective methods of parasitising other insects, ichneumon flies and chalcid-wasps have achieved a position of great importance in the field of biological control. Ladybirds, too, have been used to great effect for the same purpose. Both the larvae and the adults are predators. A species of ladybird featured in one of the very first large-scale experiments in biological control.

In 1872 a scale insect known to be a serious pest of citrus fruits was accidentally introduced from its native Australia to California. At this time orange and lemon growing was a flourishing and expanding industry in California. During the next fifteen years the pest spread to such an extent that it was threatening the whole industry with extinction. In desperation, since every known method of controlling the scale insects had been tried without success, a scientist from the United States Department of Agriculture was sent to Australia to make an intensive study of the cottony-cushion scale insect, as it was called, in order to discover whether it had any predator which might be imported into California.

He found that in Australia the scale insect was kept within bounds by a bright red ladybird, *Vedalia cardinalis*. Losing no time, he collected and despatched a number of these ladybirds to California. Just 129 arrived alive, and these were immediately released. So favourable did *Vedalia* find the climate and the abundance of food that within months millions of offspring were swarming over the citrus groves. Within two years the pest had been brought under control, and since that day only small outbreaks have occurred, and these have been quickly dealt with by the now naturalised *Vedalia*.

Much more recently the coconut scale insect, *Aspidiotus destructor*, a serious pest of the coconut palms of Fiji, has been as spectacularly overcome by the introduction of another species of ladybird, *Cryptognatha nodiceps*, from Trinidad. The first imports were made in 1928, and by the end of 1929 the pest had been brought completely under control.

It was announced in September 1970 that attempts would be made to enlist the aid of biological control to save Britain's elm trees from destruction in their thousands. The killer is the so-called Dutch elm disease, a fungus called *Ceratocystis ulmi*. Its spores are spread from tree to tree by a small beetle, *Scolytus scolytus*, and the rapid spread of the disease is due to a sudden proliferation of this beetle, which has been relatively dormant for many years. Once a tree has become infested its death is remarkably rapid.

The seriousness of this epidemic is underlined by the fact that three-fifths of all the trees in England are elms, and that some 30 per cent of these had been killed during the previous two years.

Arrangements were made to import in spring 1971 a stock of a rather rare chalcid-wasp from Austria. Some recent experiments with this wasp in Missouri seemed to indicate that it might well be able to control the spread of the beetle. At least it chooses the larva of *Scolytus scolytus* in which to lay its eggs.

CHAPTER 10

Death by Poisoning

POISON has always been regarded as the assassin's most subtle weapon, but the ability to kill by deliberate poisoning is by no means a human prerogative. Highly efficient methods of killing their prey by the injection of poisons have been evolved quite independently in several widely separated groups of animals.

In general, structural and functional efficiency increases the higher an animal is placed in the animal kingdom, yet one of the most efficient and beautifully designed structures for injecting poison to be found anywhere occurs in the coelenterates, the sea-anemones and jellyfish, which are among its most primitive members.

No animal could look more innocuous than the sea-anemone waving its tentacles gently in the shallow water of a rock pool. Yet for its size it is one of nature's most accomplished killers. If you were fortunate enough to witness a prawn or a small fish passing close enough to the anemone to brush against one or more of these tentacles you would see it stop in its tracks as though suddenly restrained by some invisible power. For a short time it may struggle, but soon all movement ceases and it is dead. Slowly the tentacles to which it now seems to be firmly attached bend inwards towards the anemone's mouth to lower the victim into its capacious stomach.

Only the microscope can show the cause of this dramatic death. Among the cells forming the walls of the tentacles are large numbers of sting cells or cnidoblasts. Within each cnidoblast there is a nematocyst, a large vacuole filled with poisonous fluid and containing also a coil of thread attached to a barbed harpoon. Projecting from the surface of the cell there is a short trigger-like process known as the cnidocil. When this is touched by the body of a passing animal the harpoon shoots violently out of the nematocyst to penetrate the body of the prey, carrying with it a small amount of poison. Because there are so many cnidoblasts on even a small area of tentacle the slightest touch releases large numbers of harpoons, which collectively inject a significant volume of poison into the victim.

The harpoon can be fired only once, so new cnidoblasts capable of moving to the surface of the tentacles to replace those which the anemone uses up every day in capturing its food are continually being developed. They occur in such numbers, especially towards the tips of the tentacles, that they have been described when seen under a microscope as 'overlying each other like herrings in a barrel'.

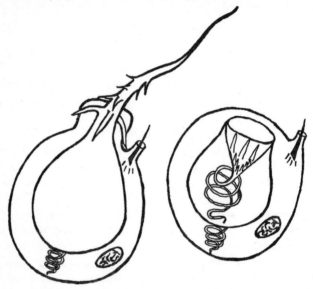

Coelenterate nematocist, discharged (left) and undischarged (right)

One of the earliest and most graphic descriptions of the powers of a sea-anemone's nematocysts was given by the great Victorian naturalist Philip Henry Gosse more than a century ago. He was out collecting on the south Devon coast one day during the 1850s, and had just put two specimens of the common opelet anenome into a jar, when he found a young conger eel about six inches long. Without thinking he put this into the jar containing the anemones.

> Before it could reach the bottom of the jar, the green tentacles of one of the Opelets had entwined themselves around its head, and, wrapping the wretch around as if with a cloth, almost in an instant had dragged it to the cavernous mouth, in which it was partially engulphed. My little son, who was with me, begged for the life of the fish, and I drew it by force from the green embrace, in less than five minutes after its capture. But it was all up with the poor eel; its eyes were already dimmed in death, and in lay in my hand flaccid and helpless, with only a momentary convulsion or two; and when I

restored it to the offended gourmand, it was speedily lost to view, coiled up in the capacious maw.

People with sensitive skin often feel a slight stinging sensation, similar to that produced by contact with a stinging nettle, when they touch anemone tentacles, and the skin may even develop similar white bumps for an hour or two.

The mechanism by which the nematocyst is released is not really understood. All that can be said is that as soon as the cnidocil is touched the fluid pressure within the cytoplasm of the cell is suddenly increased, with the result that the nematocyst bursts to expel the harpoon it contains.

Cnidoblasts precisely the same in structure as those found on sea-anemone tentacles also occur on the tentacles of jelly-fish and of the colonial siphonophores, best known of which is the Portuguese man-of-war. Many of these have formidible batteries which may cause severe pain and distress to anyone unfortunate enough to touch them. Indeed the tentacles of the Portuguese man-of-war are extremely dangerous and have been responsible for a number of deaths. A specimen six inches across is capable of killing and digesting a full-grown mackerel.

Cnidoblasts are quite clearly offensive weapons, being used by all the major coelenterate groups to capture their prey. Equally they are defensive weapons. Very few animals attack or feed upon coelenterates, and most will try to keep well out of their way. On the other hand a number of animals belonging to other groups have learned to take advantage of the protection which these coelenterate tentacles offer.

Young cod, whiting and other fish when they are about an inch long seek out one of the large jellyfish of the genus *Cyanea*, taking shelter beneath its umbrella until they have grown to several inches in length and are no longer so vulnerable to their enemies. No potential enemy will risk pursuing them beneath the umbrella, because the long tentacles of *Cyanea* are heavily armed with cnidoblasts. These jellyfish are very common all over the North Atlantic, and often attain a diameter of at least six feet. The largest specimen ever recorded had a diameter of twelve feet with trailing tentacles more than one hundred feet long. The young fish sheltering beneath these enormous umbrellas survive only by exercising care, because they have no natural immunity to jellyfish poison. If they misjudge the position of the tentacles and brush against them they end up in the jellyfish's stomach.

Among the coral reefs of Australia and other parts of the western Pacific there are large numbers of damsel fish, also known as coral fish and clown fish. They are striped in bright colours, which explains the last name. One of the most abundant of them is *Amphiprion percula*, a small fish about three inches in length with a bright orange-and-white striped body and black-tipped fins. To the biologist these coral fish are particularly interesting because of their close association with the large sea-anemones living on these reefs. Except for brief sorties in search of their prey they live among the tentacles of the anemones. Unlike young whiting and cod, however, they are apparently completely immune to the effects of nematocyst poison, because they make no attempt to avoid contact with the tentacles, frequently brushing against them as they swim around.

This is an interesting example of commensalism, the name given to the association of two kinds of animals for their mutual benefit. The benefit which the damsel fish derives is obvious, but what is the advantage to the anemone ? It has been said that when the fish eats its prey, some of the pieces are picked up by the anemone's tentacles. Whether this is true or not, there is certainly plenty of evidence that anemones with damsel fish in attendance seem to thrive more than those without such partners. Further research will no doubt throw more light on the benefits which the anemones derive from this association. One interesting fact is that each species of fish is found in association with only one or a few species of anemone, and that no species of anemone shelters more than one species of fish. The significance of these facts is not yet understood.

One of the classic examples of commensalism is the partnership between various species of hermit crabs and sea-anemones. The hermit crab, having lost the protective shell from all parts of its body except the front end, lives with its abdomen tucked permanently within an empty mollusc shell, the size of which depends upon the state of development of the crab. When it is young a winkle or top shell will give it adequate accommodation, but when it has attained full size it makes its home in a discarded whelk shell.

The largest of the British hermit crabs, and the one most common in seashore rock pools, is *Eupagurus bernhardus*. Fully grown it lives in a discarded whelk shell, on the top of which there will almost invariably be a sea-anemone of the species *Calliactus parasitica*. From this association both partners can be shown to derive some advantage. The crab gains because the anemone warns off potential predators which will not risk coming into contact with the anemone's batteries of nematocysts in an attempt to attack the crab which it is covering. The anemone gains by being carried around to a variety of feeding grounds and

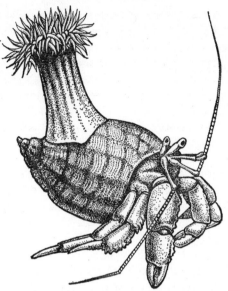

A hermit crab living in its adopted whelk shell which bears the crab's
anemone partner

this increases its chances of finding suitable prey. As the crab breaks up
its own food, too, the anemone will often bend down so that its tentacles
can pick up some of the scraps.

There is plenty of evidence to suggest that these associations between
hermit crabs and sea-anemones are consciously achieved by both
parties. When a growing crab has to change its shell for a larger one it
has been observed to detach its attendant anemone and place it carefully
on the new shell. On the other hand an anemone put into an aquarium
tank containing a number of empty crab shells will not usually settle on
any of them, apparently preferring to fix itself to the glass. If a hermit
crab is then introduced into the tank it will choose one of the shells for
its home, and before long the anemone will have moved from the glass
to the top of the shell.

The tropical crab *Melia tessalata* uses sea-anemones for its own
defence in the most positive manner. It is not a hermit crab and therefore has no borrowed shell on which it can carry its partners. Instead it
carries an anemone in each of its claws, and when approached by a
potential enemy it holds the anemones so that their formidable rings of
tentacles face the would-be predator. It is said that if the crab comes
across a larger anemone than one of those which it is carrying, it will
detach it from its rock and leave the smaller specimen in its place.

One family of sea-slugs, the Aeoliidae, has achieved ultimate perfection in the art of using coelenterate nematocysts for its own defence.
In common with other families of sea-slugs the Aeoliidae feed upon sea-
anemones and other sedentary coelenterates. As a group the sea-slugs
are apparently immune to the effects of nematocyst poison. The remarkable thing about the aeoliids is that when they swallow coelenterate
tissues the cnidoblasts remain intact despite coming into contact with
the walls of their digestive system. From the main part of the gut
numerous tubules lead up towards the dorsal surface of the body to end
in club-shaped swellings all along the back, and it is in these cerata, as
they are called, that the cnidoblasts collect. Here they provide a most
effective deterrent to any would-be enemies of the slugs. The aeoliids
are thus as effectively protected by the cnidoblasts as the coelenterates
from which they have 'borrowed' them.

The twenty or so phyla or major groups into which the animal kingdom
is divided are very unequal both in the number of species they contain
and in the total number of individuals belonging to them. By far the
largest is the phylum Arthropoda, to which more than three-quarters of
all the animal species at present known to science belong. It is divided
into five sub-phyla, the Crustacea (shrimps, prawns, crabs, lobsters,
waterfleas, barnacles, woodlice, etc.), the Chilopoda (centipedes), the
Diplopoda (millipedes), the Arachnida (spiders, scorpions, mites and
ticks) and the Insecta. Spiders, scorpions and centipedes all have well
developed mechanisms for injecting poison into their prey and their
enemies, and the effect of some of them can be painful and even dangerous to man.

In contrast to the insects with their many pairs of mouth parts on the
head segments, the spiders have only two pairs of head appendages, the
first being a pair of jaws or chelicerae, which are the poison fangs, and
the second a pair of palpi. Each fang consists of two parts, a wide basal
segment and a sharp-pointed curved terminal claw. The inner edge of
the basal segment is toothed, and the claw can be folded back against it
in much the same way as the blade of a penknife folds into its handle.
Within each side of the head, internal to the basal segment, is a poison
gland surrounded by muscles. Their contractions force the venom into a
tube which runs right through the two segments of the chelicera to open
at the tip of the claw. By means of this mechanism the victim receives
a hypodermic injection of poison as soon as the jaws penetrate its body.

Although all spiders possess these poison fangs which enable them to
paralyse their prey, only a tiny minority is able to cause serious distress

to man, and these few have become notorious. The most dangerous of these are the tarantula of Italy, the black widow of North America, the Australian black susan and trap-door spiders, all relatively small spiders, and the giant bird-eating spiders of South America.

Like the spiders, the scorpions also possess a weapon designed to give a hypodermic injection of poison to their victims. This time, however, it is the terminal segment of the very flexible abdomen which has become modified as a formidable sting. Although it is only a single pear-shaped structure ending in a sharp curved spine, ducts from two separate poison glands housed in the body of the sting open at the tip of the spine.

The poison fangs of the Chilopoda or centipedes are not comparable in origin with those of the spiders. Whereas in the spiders they belong to the head, in the centipedes they represent the modified appendages of the first body or trunk segment. Despite this their structure and method of functioning are similar.

Each consists of a sharp, curved claw attached to a much wider basal section, these two being similar to the claw and basal section of a spider's fangs. Both are attached to a single plate within the body segment. Two poison glands situated within the segment connect with the tips of the claws by means of a tube through which the venom is discharged.

The total number of people who die annually from poisoning by coelenterates, insects and arachnids is very small. The vast majority of deaths caused by animal poisoning are due to snake bite, the total number of such deaths amounting to thousands every year. A survey made in 1954 suggested that the figure might be as high as 40,000, the majority of which occur in India and south-east Asia. Even so it is only a small proportion of the snakes of the world which produce a venom virulent enough to kill. A good many others are capable of causing pain and swelling without being ultimately dangerous. But nearly all snakes can be classified as harmless, the limit of their effect when they do bite being no more than the perforations which their teeth produce when breaking the skin.

From the early days of their evolution from the lizards snakes developed in two quite different directions. The first type developed and perfected the method of coiling round its prey, crushing the life out of it by preventing it from breathing. These snakes grew large, developed powerful muscles and produced eventually the massive pythons, boas and anacondas which constitute the modern group of constricting snakes forming the family Boidae.

The alternative line of evolution centred around the production of saliva which poisoned or at least paralysed the animals' prey. At first the saliva was just mildly toxic to the small animals which constituted the snakes' food, a condition represented today by the thousand or so species of snakes usually called harmless. The description is apt if one compares them with the later products of evolution in this direction, for in these snakes there is no definite poison apparatus, the slightly toxic saliva entering haphazardly into the wounds inflicted by the teeth.

From this point two separate lines of evolution led to the modern venomous snakes. In one group grooves were developed in some of the back teeth of the upper jaw and down these channels the saliva, now somewhat more potent, trickled into the wound. The harmless and the back-fanged snakes are closely related, constituting between them the single family Colubridæ, which contains more than half the total living species of snakes. Although some of the back-fanged snakes are capable of giving a painful bite, the only species which can really be said to be dangerous to man is the African boomslang, *Dispholidus typus*.

Parallel with the development of the back-fanged snakes, another group evolved a much more efficient poison apparatus. This time it was the front teeth of the upper jaw which became modified as saliva channels. At first the teeth were grooved, but later, in some species, the groove became covered to form a tube. At the same time muscles developed around the salivary glands, so that by their contraction the saliva, becoming ever more potent, could be forced under pressure through these hollow fangs into the wound. The perfection of this method is exemplified by our modern cobras, kraits, coral snakes, and mambas. All of these are exceedingly poisonous, and their bite is almost certain to be fatal to man unless appropriate antidotes are available. These front-fanged poisonous snakes belong to the family Elapidae.

Their fangs are fairly short and permanently erected. Elapid snakes are generally thin, rather long and very active, some being capable of considerable turns of speed. Their distribution is almost world-wide, Europe being the only continent in which they are not represented.

Although they all produce a poisonous venom, many of the elapids are not very dangerous. The numerous coral snakes of the New World, for example, are docile by nature and secretive in their habits, and will not attempt to strike unless actually stepped on or handled, though their venom is extremely potent. A bite will generally prove fatal within twenty-four hours unless the victim is treated.

No other group of venomous snakes claims such an appalling number of victims as the various specimens of cobras, especially in India. It has been estimated that some 200,000 people are bitten by snakes every year in India, the majority by cobras; of these some 15,000 die. The group has representatives in Africa and southern Asia. Nine species are found in Africa, the best known being the Egyptian cobra, *Naja haja*, with a range extending also into the adjacent parts of Africa. Equally famous or notorious is the Indian cobra, *Naja naja*, which has a wide range covering the Indian subcontinent and the Malay archipelago to the Philippines.

Despite the often repeated stories of venomous snakes chasing people in order to bite them, the fact remains that most snakes, both harmless and venomous, will avoid man if they possibly can. Given sufficient warning of his approach they will prefer to slide off into the undergrowth rather than face him. Only if they are suddenly disturbed at close quarters, or are trodden or sat upon, will most of them attempt to strike. Even when approached closely their apparent intention to strike is more often than not a bluff, an actual strike occurring only when they feel themselves imminently threatened. The one notable exception is the largest of all the venomous snakes, the king cobra or hamadryad, *Naja hannah*, of India and south-east Asia. This snake grows to a maximum length of about eighteen feet, and has the reputation of attacking unprovoked. It is, too, unusual in its feeding habits, eating only other snakes unless driven to severe hunger to make do with less desirable food as a temporary measure.

All snakes are great bluffers, and none more so than the venomous species. The cobra when roused has a more formidable appearance than any other type, with its sinister hood spread out just behind its head. This is really a fold of loose skin on either side of the head extended by a series of movable ribs whenever the creature is roused.

Not only are snakes less ready to strike than popular belief would have us think, but when they do bite the results are not always as serious as is generally supposed. Only if the snake gets in a really good strike will the fangs sink far enough to inject a full dose of venom. In most cases they will do little more than graze the skin, injecting only a partial dose. In these instances the victim will in all probability recover without treatment.

Much has been written about the battles between cobras and various species of mongoose. Most small mammals fall fairly easy prey to the cobra when it is out hunting at night, but during the daytime there is evidence that its sight is not particularly good. Cobras under observation have been seen to strike many times at a small agile mammal without scoring a hit. The mongoose probably owes its superiority over the cobra to a combination of extreme agility and its habit of raising its thick fur when roused. This makes it appear bigger than it really is, and if the snake manages to strike at all it strikes short and fails to reach the skin. In Africa and Asia mongooses are often kept as pets to keep houses free of snakes.

Some cobras are known as spitting cobras from their ability to send out a spray of venom in two fine jets for a distance of a yard or two. These spitters are extremely accurate in their aim, and always direct the jets at the eyes of their victims. The purpose of this is obscure, because although the venom may cause temporary blindness it is incapable of causing death. It has been suggested that the spraying is a means of warning off large grazing animals which might otherwise trample on and kill the cobras. In order to be able to send out these jets the fangs of the spitting cobras are modified. Instead of opening at the tips of the fangs the venom ducts open towards the front of them just above their tips, so that as the venom is forced through the fangs it emerges as a forward jet.

The reputation of the mambas of Africa is rather like that of the cobras in Africa and Asia, and equally exaggerated. They are indeed dangerous snakes, being extremely agile and able to raise a relatively large part of the body above the ground when they strike. This makes it easier for them to deliver bites in the body region, where treatment is more difficult, than a bite located on the limbs. They are also arboreal in their habits, which often gives them the opportunity of attacking from above. There are five species, of which the largest and most deadly is the black mamba, *Dendroaspis polylepis*, which can attain a length of fourteen feet. Although the adults are dark brown or black, young specimens are green, and are consequently often confused with the much smaller green mamba, *Dendroaspis angusticeps*. The other three species are less common and much more restricted in their distribution.

The group of front-fanged venomous snakes is completed with the kraits, brilliantly coloured, dangerous snakes of south-east Asia, and several Australian poisonous snakes, the most important being the taipan, *Oxyuranus scutellatus*, most deadly of all the Australian snakes, which is said to attack on sight and to have a bite which is almost invariably fatal; the tiger snake, *Notechis scutatus*, less deadly than the taipan but usually said to be the most dangerous snake in Australia because it is a much more common species; the death adder *Acanthophis antarcticus*, which has a thick-set body and broad head much more like a typical viper than a front-fanged snake; and the black snake, *Pseudechis porphyriacus*, best known because of the fierce fights between males at the breeding season.

The sea-snakes, comprising the family Hydrophiidae, are similar to the Elapidae, and were probably derived from them. They show several structural modifications in adaptation to their aquatic mode of life. The tail is flattened from side to side, and the body slightly so. The nostrils are situated on the top of the snout, and the nasal passages are provided with valves so that they can be closed to exclude water. The ventral scales have been lost in most species, and this makes it difficult for them to move about efficiently on land.

Recent research has shown that the sea-snakes produce a more potent venom than any other snake, yet curiously they are virtually harmless. They apparently never attack bathers, and their fang mechanism is not very efficient. They feed almost exclusively on fish, and are particularly partial to eels.

During the evolution of the front-fanged snakes a second group of highly poisonous snakes was evolving from back-fanged ancestors. The maxillae, the bones bearing all the teeth including the poison fangs, were progressively shortened from behind, while the teeth in front of the fangs were gradually reduced in number until finally none of them remained. In this way the fangs, like those of the front-fanged snakes, came to lie at the front of the mouth, the idea position for striking. Unlike the fangs of the elapids they can be folded back along the upper jaw when not in use. They are considerably longer than elapid fangs.

This group of snakes, representing the latest development in snake evolution, constitutes the family Viperidae, the vipers. Their saliva is every bit as deadly as that of the Elapidae. Included in the family are the true vipers, the puff adders and the rattlesnakes, the latter forming a special group known as pit vipers, so-called because a pit of unknown function forms a depression between the eyes and the nostrils.

In contrast to the Elapidae, the Viperidae are mostly thick-set snakes with broad flattened heads. Of the true vipers the best known are the common adder or viper, *Vipera berus*, which is found in almost every part of Europe, including Britain; the puff adder, *Bitis lachesis*, which is widespread in Africa and Arabia; the African gaboon viper, *Bitis gabonica;* and the deadly Russell's viper, *Vipera russelli*, of southern Asia.

The pit vipers are of two kinds, the rattlesnakes and those without rattles. The most important members of the latter group are the American moccasins and copperheads, *Agkistrodon* species, the highly venemous fer-de-lance, *Bothrops atrox*, of South America, and the bushmaster, *Lachesis muta*, of tropical America, the largest of all the pit vipers, which grows to a maximum length of twelve feet.

Twenty-eight species of rattlesnakes are recognised, all coming from North, Central and South America. The rattle, formed from several modified tail bones, is thought by some authorities to serve a similar purpose to the venom of the spitting cobras, to warn off large animals which might otherwise tread on the snakes and kill them.

Snake venoms are of two different types. One type acts on the nervous system, paralysing the centres controlling the working of the heart or of the breathing mechanism. Most of the Elapidae and Hydrophiidae produce a venom of this type, known as neurotoxic, whereas the majority of the Viperidae produce a quite different type of venom which destroys the blood and the small blood vessels. This type of venom is described as haemotoxic or haemorrhagic.

The belief that a shrew's bite is poisonous dates back to early folklore, and was dismissed by modern zoologists along with the jewel which was supposed to be in the toad's head and numerous other curiosities of popular superstition. But wholesale discarding of long-held beliefs can itself lead to error, for experiments begun in 1942 on an American species of shrew *Blarina brevicaudata*, showed that the saliva of this species had in fact powerful toxic properties.

Shrews have two pairs of salivary glands, a pair of parotid glands in the cheeks and a pair of submaxillary glands at the back of the mouth. Extracts of various strengths from the two kinds of glands were injected into a variety of small mammals with spectacular results. Parotid-gland extracts proved quite harmless, but those of the submaxillary glands were astonishingly potent and deadly. An amount of submaxillary-gland extract equivalent to fifteen-millionths of the victim's body weight was sufficient to kill most mice within a quarter of an hour, while four times this dosage was fatal to all mice within six minutes. An equivalent dose injected into a rabbit killed it in five minutes. The shrew poison seems to act in the same way as the venom produced by the cobras and other elapid snakes, affecting the nervous system and causing paralysis and respiratory failure.

Poison is a chemical weapon and usually, as we have seen in this chapter, it can kill. Certain animals, however, have developed the ability to produce chemicals in the form of scents which, even if they are not lethal, can at least be used to protect.

Scent glands and the secretions produced by them play an important part in the lives of all carnivores. These secretions are particularly strong, and most of them are objectionable to our sense of smell while some of them, for example that of the skunk, are quite intolerable. As with the other mammals the scent of the carnivore is used for two purposes. In the first place it serves to lay a trail, and so enables the sexes to locate each other at the breeding season, an important consideration with animals which generally lead solitary lives; or in the case of gregarious species it enables the members of a group to keep together. It is also used for marking out territory, and so to warn off other members of the same species straying from their own domains.

Small carnivores kept in zoos always mark the boundaries of their cages with these secretions, which explains why the houses in which they are exhibited usually have an objectionable smell. It is impossible to keep them sweet, for as soon as the cages are cleaned and the scent removed the occupants go round the cages to renew their marks.

Birds and mammals all possess sebaceous or oil glands to produce the oily secretions which are spread over hair and feathers to keep them supple and waterproof. The scent glands of the carnivorous mammals are a pair of these sebaceous glands situated at either side of the base of the tail which are much enlarged and modified to produce the special scent secretion.

Among British mammals the polecat is known for the potency of its particularly obnoxious scent which, however, is mild compared with that of the skunk. Whether any other carnivores use their secretions actively to discourage attacks from their enemies may be disputed, but there is certainly no doubt that the skunk does appreciate the power of its scent as a protective weapon. Charles Darwin, in his famous account of the voyage of the *Beagle*, described the skunk's ability to deter.

We saw also a couple of Zorillos, or skunks – odious animals, which are far from uncommon. In general appearance the Zorillo resembles a polecat, but it is rather larger, and much thicker in proportion. Conscious of its power, it roams by day about the open plain, and fears neither dog nor man. If a dog is urged to the attack, its courage is instantly checked by a few drops of the fetid oil, which brings on violent sickness and running at the nose. Whatever is once polluted by it is for ever useless. Azara [his South American guide] says the smell can be perceived at a league distance; more than once, when entering the harbour at Monte Video, the wind being off shore, we have perceived the odour on board the *Beagle*. Certain it is that every animal most willingly makes room for the Zorillo.

W. H. Hudson, another distinguished British naturalist who did much during the last century to make South American natural history known to the world, gives a graphic description of the social effects of the skunk. He is describing the experiences of a settler who sets off one evening on horseback to ride to a neighbour's house for a dance to which he has been invited.

E

It is a dark windy evening, but there is a convenient bridle path through the dense thicket of giant thistles, and striking it he puts his horse into a swinging gallop. Unhappily the path is already occupied by a skunk, invisible in the darkness, that, in obedience to the promptings of its insane instinct, refuses to get out of it, until the flying hoofs hit it and send it, like a well-kicked football, into the thistles. But the fore feet of the horse, up as high as his knees, perhaps, have been sprinkled, and the rider, after coming out into the open dismounts and walks away twenty yards from his animal, and literally smells himself all over, and with a feeling of profound relief pronounces himself clean. Not the minutest drop of the diabolical spray has touched his dancing-shoes.

Springing into the saddle, he proceeds to his journey's end, and is warmly welcomed by his host. In a little while people begin exchanging whispers and significant glances; ladies cough and put their handkerchiefs to their noses, and presently begin to feel faint and retire from the room. Our hero begins to notice that there is something wrong, and presently discovers its cause; he, unhappily, has been the last person to remark that familiar but most abominable odour, rising like a deadly exhalation from the floor, conquering all other odours, and every moment becoming more powerful. A drop has touched his shoe after all.

Shrews possess glands which produce a scent so strong that it seems to make them distasteful to dogs, cats and other mammals. The function of these glands, however, is probably not protection against enemies but to provide a means of marking their territories and runs and so warn off other shrews. This would help to prevent squabbles which would certainly occur if two individuals came face to face. The theory that the function of shrew scent is to keep individuals apart is supported by the fact that at the breeding season the females cease producing scent, and consequently at this time the males are not warned off. Even at other times females never produce so much scent as males. Whether or not scent plays any part in protecting shrews from their mammal enemies, it would certainly be ineffective against birds, because they have little or no sense of smell. In fact birds, and especially owls, are the shrews' chief enemies.

Perhaps the most unusual use of scent is found in a primitive Africa primate, the potto *Perodicticus potto*, a nocturnal creature which lives among the branches of trees and becomes active at night when it moves around in search of the insects and fruits which constitute its food.

These pottos are capable of exuding a strong odour originating from glands situated near their sexual organs. These secretions are quite possibly used for territory marking, though this at present is unconfirmed. One thing they undoubtedly do is to attract various night-flying flies and moths to the neighbourhood of the potto, and thus provide it with an easily obtained meal.

A number of insects can emit pungent odours designed to deter their enemies. One of the best known of these is the bombardier beetle, *Brachinus crepitans*, which when pursued emits a small quantity of an extremely volatile corrosive liquid the vapour of which is capable of heading off a potential enemy. Release of the liquid is accompanied by a distinctly audible explosive 'crack'.

Many of the brightly coloured saw-fly caterpillars emit extremely unpleasant odours when disturbed. In one species, *Croesus septentrionalis*, the hind end of the body is turned forward over the top of the head to make the discharge more effective. Many plant bugs and carabid beetles produce evil-smelling secretions when handled, while the green-metallic beetle known as the Spanish fly (*Lytta vesicatoria*) produces a deterrent liquid capable of producing blisters. The active substance it contains is known as cantharidin, and was once used by the pharmacist.

The large red wood ant, *Formica rufa*, which builds its conspicuous nests a yard of more across in pine woods, cannot sting. Instead it defends itself effectively by discharging a tiny stream of formic acid from the end of its abdomen for distances of up to twelve inches. When alarmed or annoyed the workers stand on the tips of their legs, curve their abdomens forward beneath their bodies and fire the irritant liquid at the approaching enemy. If a nest is disturbed thousands of ants will rush out to defend it, and the whole atmosphere for some distance will be pungent with the fumes of formic acid. Any ant coming into contact with the intruder is capable of giving a painful bite with its powerful jaws, injecting formic acid into the wound.

The caterpillars of the puss moth, *Dicranura vinula*, are also equipped with a mechanism enabling them to eject a spray containing formic acid. They use this defence mechanism particularly against ichneumon flies seeking to lay their eggs upon them.

A considerable number of beetles have the unusual ability to exude small drops of blood when seized, and this blood has burning properties. The blood is discharged at the limb joints. The best known practitioners of this method of defence are the ladybirds, the bloody-nosed beetles and the oil beetles.

CHAPTER II

Electricity — The Secret Weapon

To the layman the production of powerful electric shocks must seem one of the extremes of animal magic. In fact it is now known that a considerable number of quite unrelated types of fish produce electric impulses which are passed into the water surrounding them. In a few cases the discharge is of the order of several hundred volts. Such powerful discharges are capable of giving quite severe shocks to man and other large animals, and of stunning or even killing prey.

Until recently this information constituted most of what was known about the production of electricity by fishes. The value of this ability to the few species capable of producing high-voltage discharges was obvious, but the advantage to a very much larger number of species able to produce only low-voltage discharges much too weak to be of any use in catching prey remained a mystery, as did the structure and method of functioning of the various electric organs.

From the evolutionary point of view, it was difficult to understand how electric organs capable of producing discharges of several hundred volts could have been evolved.

Research over the past few decades, however, has gone a long way towards elucidating the whole phenomenon of electricity production by fishes, and has brought to light a highly sophisticated physiological adaptation of extreme importance to those species in which it is found.

Satisfactory investigation of the low-voltage discharges which are now known to be produced by a surprisingly large number of different fish species became possible only after the last war. Their detection and measurement required highly sensitive amplifiers and cathode-ray oscillographs, and these became available as a result of intensive wartime electronic research.

One of the pioneers using these extremely sensitive instruments was Dr Hans Lissmann of Cambridge University. During an expedition to Ghana he found that the very muddy waters of the rivers could be alive with electricity. This he discovered by suspending an amplifier in the water and connecting it by two insulated copper wires to an oscillograph, in which case the discharges registered on the screen, or on a pair of very sensitive headphones, when they produced a series of clicks and crackles.

Five different kinds of discharge could be distinguished, but it was upon one of these that Dr Lissmann concentrated his further investigations. This particular discharge consisted of a steady series of pulses produced at a rate of about 300 per second. It was not long before he identified the producer of this steady hum as *Gymnarchus niloticus*, a common fresh-water species found in the Nile, as its name suggests, and in many other muddy African rivers and streams.

Gymnarchus is a fish of reasonable size, which may attain a length of several feet. Its eyes are very poorly developed and would probably be of little use even in clear waters. In the muddy waters it inhabits they must be quite useless. Yet it feeds exclusively on other fish which are themselves capable of rapid movement. Dr Lissmann was also impressed by its navigational abilities. Under close observation it was seen frequently to swim backwards into crevices without once colliding with the sides.

One other observation, the significance of which we shall see later, was that whereas most fish propel themselves through the water by means of powerful side-to-side undulations of the body and tail, *Gymnarchus* keeps its body completely straight at all times, relying for propulsion solely upon the exceptionally well-developed dorsal fin running almost the whole length of the dorsal surface of the fish. By contrast the caudal, anal and pelvic fins are not developed, so that the tail tapers to a point.

Armed with all this information Dr Lissmann evolved his theory that *Gymnarchus* uses its electric field both as a means of navigation and also in order to detect and capture its prey. To examine his theory he devised a series of experiments conducted upon specimens of *Gymnarchus* kept in an aquarium tank.

First he placed a vertical board of plywood outside the tank and brought up a bar magnet which he moved about behind the plywood so that the fish could not see it. The fish responded, however, and as the magnet was moved up and down or backwards and forwards behind the screen, so the fish followed it on the other side. Other materials such as slate and marble were also used to form the vertical screen, and in each case the results were the same. Only a metal screen failed to evoke any response when the magnet was moved.

The results of these experiments led to the theory that the constant electric field with which *Gymnarchus* surrounds itself enables it to detect and capture its prey, and also to avoid colliding with obstacles. The electric field would be distorted by any other fish or any obstacle coming within it and thus betray its presence. In other words *Gymnarchus* detects its prey by a process remarkably similar to radar, itself an electrical detection device invented by man in the 1930s but now revealed to have originated with fish many millions of years earlier.

The electric field produced by *Gymnarchus* probably also provides a means of communicating with other members of its own species. In a further series of experiments six pairs of electrodes were installed at intervals around the sides of the tank. The electrical discharges of a specimen were then recorded and 'played back' through one of these electrodes. Whichever electrode was used to return the discharges was vigorously attacked. This suggests that in the river each individual's electric field serves to warn off other members of the species from its territory. It is well known that specimens of *Gymnarchus* are quarrelsome among themselves and cannot live satisfactorily together in the same aquarium tank.

The rigid body of *Gymnarchus* is now seen to be a necessity in an animal producing around itself a constant electrical field. Any distortion of the body would automatically distort the field.

Along with the research into the behaviour of electric fishes there has been corresponding work on the structure of the electric organs, so that much is now known about how these fish produce their electricity. The electric organs of *Gymnarchus* consist of eight tubular structures, four on each side stretching from the tip of the tail right through the tail region. Each of these organs consists of a considerable number of electroplates representing modified muscle cells. Each electroplate has

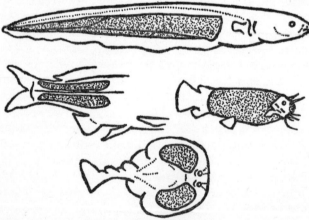

Various positions of electric organs in fish. Above: electric eel. Middle left: morymyroid fish. Middle right: electric cat-fish. Bottom: electric torpedo.

the shape of a vertical disc, one face being flat and supplied with a nerve fibre, while the other is deeply folded. All the plates fit closely together like a pile of coins laid on its side. Each organ contains between 150 and 200 electroplates, making a total of between 1,200 and 1,600 altogether. Each electroplate is embedded in a gelatinous matrix, giving the whole organ a clear jelly-like appearance.

Gymnarchus is one of a group of mormyroid fishes. All are freshwater species confined to the rivers and other fresh waters of tropical Africa. Recent investigations have shown that all of them have electric organs. Altogether there are about 150 species, all except *Gymnarchus* possessing only a pair of electric organs on either side of the tail, and the total number of electroplates is thus between 600 and 800.

Assuming that these mormyroid fish do use their electric organs for detecting prey in muddy waters and the approach of members of their own species, then they must also have some means of detecting changes in their electric field which the approach of these other fish will cause.

Much less is known about the electric sense organs than about the organs producing electricity. The skin of mormyroid fishes, however, is pitted with large numbers of pores. Each pore leads into a jelly-filled canal at the bottom of which is a sense organ known as a mormyromast. The nerves from these mormyromasts all go to a specially enlarged part of the brain cerebellum, which is relatively much larger than in most other fish. As yet there is no positive proof that these mormyromasts are indeed capable of detecting changes in the electric field. On the other hand it does not seem possible to assign any other function to them, and although other electric fishes possess similar organs they have not been found in any species of fish which is not known to be electric.

No mormyroids are found outside Africa nor, so far as we know, have mormyroids ever existed elsewhere at any time. In the rivers and lakes of Central and South America, however, there is found a group of knife-fishes whose whole electric behaviour is strikingly similar to that of the mormyroids. Yet the two groups belong to two entirely different orders. They cannot therefore have inherited their electric abilities from a common electric ancestor. The two electric systems must have been evolved quite separately.

In addition to his invaluable researches into the electric behaviour of the mormyroids Dr Lissmann was the first to discover the electrogenic abilities of a knife-fish, *Gymnotus carapo*. This species, like the mormyroids, could detect a moving magnet and follow it. Since this discovery a team of American zoologists has investigated a number of knife fishes, and every one so far examined has proved to be electrogenic. It seems likely that they will eventually all be found to possess the ability.

The knife-fishes are so named because they have extremely thin triangular-shaped bodies, deep at the front end and tapering to a point at the end of the tail. Just as with the mormyroids, only one fin is developed, but in this case it is not the dorsal but the anal fin, and this extends almost the whole length of the body and tail. The dorsal and caudal fins are suppressed.

Again, like the mormyroids, the knife-fishes keep their bodies rigid, all movement resulting from the undulations of the anal fin, to avoid distortion of the electric field produced by the electric organs. These organs are similar in structure to those of the mormyroids, and are derived from the outer portions of the trunk and tail muscles. Knife-fishes also possess sense organs similar in structure to the mormyro-masts of the mormyroids, and their nerve supply, too, comes from the cerebellum, which is likewise greatly enlarged.

Recent research has also shown that, like the mormyroids, the knife-fishes can travel forwards or backwards with equal ease, and that when travelling backwards at speed they pass through small openings without ever touching the sides, a feat which could not be accomplished even with the most acute sight.

It seems likely that each mormyroid and knife-fish species produces its own characteristic electric field. The American investigators found that electric impulses were emitted with remarkable regularity by all species, and that it made no difference whether the fish were actively swimming or resting upon the bottom of their aquarium tank. For example *Gymnotus* was found to produce impulses at the rate of about 65 per second, *Gymnorhumpichthys* at about 100 per second, and *Eigenmannia* at about 300 per second. The maximum voltage recorded has never exceeded three-tenths of a volt.

In contrast to the mormyroids and knife-fishes, whose electrogenic capabilities have been revealed only comparatively recently, the production of high-voltage electrical discharges by the electric eel, *Electrophorus electricus*, has been known for a very long time. Despite its name it is not an eel. In fact it belongs to a different order, and is quite closely related to the knife-fishes, being like them a native of Central and South American rivers where the waters are often extremely muddy. It also keeps its body rigid and moves by means of undulations of its enormously developed anal fin, the dorsal and caudal fins being undeveloped.

Electric eels grow to a length of at least eight feet. Until they are about one foot long they have quite normal eyes, but thereafter their eyes degenerate and they become blind.

The electric eel is undoubtedly the most spectacular of all the electric fishes. Its powerful discharge is capable of giving a severe shock to humans, and of stunning and even killing large fish. Measurements have shown that these discharges may attain a voltage of 650 with a current strength of up to one amp.

Incidentally it seems likely that the electric eel likes to eat its prey alive, and that it therefore adjusts the strength of its high-voltage discharge according to the size of its victim so that it is merely stunned and not killed. It has been observed in an aquarium tank that an electric eel will not eat a fish which it has killed, but will readily swallow a stunned one.

Recent research into other electric fishes led to a more thorough investigation of electricity production in the electric eel, with surprising results. Studies of electric eels kept at the New York Aquarium revealed that while they were lying on the bottom of the tank there was no electrical activity but as soon as they started to swim about small electric discharges comparable to those produced by the mormyroids and knife-fishes could be detected. These were quite different both in nature and in power from the familiar high-voltage discharges used to stun prey, and which were also produced if the fish was disturbed. The powerful pulses were repeated several times a second, each pulse lasting for about three milliseconds, but the low-voltage discharges were produced at the rate of about fifty per second.

Examination of the electric organs revealed that these were more elaborate than those of the previous two groups. They are developed from the lower parts of the muscle segments of the tail, and consist in fact of three distinct elements. Throughout most of the length of the tail lies the main organ, which is responsible for producing the high-voltage discharges. Behind this is a second much smaller organ, known as the organ of Sachs, and it is this organ which produces the low-voltage discharges. Beneath both organs is a third small electric organ, the function of which is as yet unknown.

As with the mormyroids and the knife-fishes, the electric organs of the electric eel are composed of electroplates, those of the main organ being packed more closely than those of the other two organs. The main structure consists of about 70 columns of electroplates along each side of the tail, each column containing between six and ten thousand separate electroplates. The tail itself comprises much more than half the total body of the electric eel. In fact the electric organs alone constitute about half the total body weight.

It is now clear that the weak electric discharges already mentioned are produced by the organ of Sachs, and their function is precisely the same as that of the low-voltage discharges produced by the electric organs of the mormyroids and the knife-fishes, namely to locate prey swimming in the vicinity. Whereas members of these groups have to capture the detected prey by normal means, however, the electric eel has developed a second, more powerful, type of electric organ to capture the prey which its weaker organs have located.

Virtually nothing is known concerning the sense organs with which the electric eel receives the information provided by its organ of Sachs. Experiments have established however that if the head of an electric eel is covered with lacquer it is incapable of receiving such information and therefore of detecting its prey even though it is producing electric discharges normally. Clearly then such electric sense organs as it possesses must be located in the head.

Just as the African mormyroids have their counterparts in the similar but quite unrelated knife-fishes of Central and South America, so the South American electric eels have their tropical African counterparts in the electric catfishes, *Malapterurus electricus*. These have not yet been subject to modern research techniques, but it is known that a four-foot specimen can produce a discharge of something like 350 volts, making the catfish perhaps second only to the electric eel in its capacity to produce high voltage electricity. Such a discharge is of course sufficient to stun large fish, and it seems likely that the catfish uses this power to capture its prey. Whether it is also capable of producing a low-voltage electric field in order to locate its prey is as yet unknown, but by analogy with the other three groups previously considered it seems more than likely. It certainly lives in muddy water, and its eyes are not particularly well developed.

The electric organs of the catfish are placed further forward than in most other groups of electric fishes, being situated beneath the skin of the trunk and the fore part of the tail. As in all other groups they represent modified muscle cells, and consist of electroplates of the usual structure.

So far as the present state of knowledge goes all the groups of electrogenic fresh-water fishes have now been considered, though of course it is not impossible that further research may reveal other electrogenic groups in other parts of the world. It is perhaps significant that all known electrogenic fresh-water fish come either from tropical Africa or Central and South America. None are known from any other part of the world.

All the electrogenic fresh-water fishes are bony fishes, but of the marine examples one group are bony: the stargazers. These small fish, seldom exceeding a foot in length, are rather sluggish in their habits, usually lying on the sea-bed waiting for their prey. Their small eyes

facing upwards give them their common name. They are widely
distributed in the western Atlantic and the eastern Pacific.

Unlike other electrogenic fishes, whose electric organs are developed
from modified trunk or tail muscles, the electric organs of the stargazer
are formed from a modification of some of its eye muscles, and so are
situated just behind the eyes in the head region. Nothing more is so far
known about the electric activities of the stargazers, as it has not yet
been possible to investigate these in specimens living in aquarium
tanks. But it is known that the charges produced can be felt by the
human hand, so it is possible that they may be used by the fish to
capture their prey.

We now come to the last two groups of electrogenic fish, the torpedo
rays and the skates. These are distantly related forms. Both belong to
the great group of cartilaginous fishes, which group also includes the
sharks. The skates and rays are flat fish in which the body is flattened
from top to bottom, in contrast to the bony flatfish, the plaice, soles,
turbot, halibut, etc., in which the bodies are flattened from side to side.
They are distinguished by the possession of two well-developed 'wings'.
In the torpedo rays the bulk of each wing is occupied by a gelatinous
electric organ, in which the electroplates are arranged in vertical piles.

Like all skates and rays, torpedo rays are rather sluggish fish which
spend their time on the sea-bed, most of them feeding on small molluscs
and crustacea which are easy to capture. The torpedo rays, however,
feed upon very active fish. The stomachs of full-grown specimens of
Torpedo nobiliana, which reach a length of six feet, have been found to
contain four-pound salmon, two-pound eels, flounders, red mullet,
plaice and spotted dogfish. It can only be assumed that in order to
capture these fish, many of which are swift movers, the torpedo ray must
have made use of its electric abilities. Indeed specimens of this particular species have been shown to produce discharges of up to 220 volts.

Whether all the skates possess electric organs is not yet known but
many of them certainly do. They are situated in the tail, and are formed
from modified tail muscles. They are not capable of producing high
voltages, the most powerful discharges recorded so far being attributable
to the thorn-back ray, *Raia clavata*, which can produce a discharge of
about four volts. Nothing is known for certain of the way in which
these skates employ their electricity.

Apart from their intrinsic interest in possessing such an unusual
ability, the various kinds of electrogenic fishes provide a most striking
example of convergent evolution. As has already been shown the various
groups of electric fishes could not have derived their abilities by descent

from one another or from a common ancestor, because they have no such ancestor. The only two groups which probably owe their electrogenic powers to a common ancestor are the knife-fishes and the electric eel.

Thus electric powers have been developed independently along at least six separate lines of evolution to produce the mormyroids, the knife-fishes and electric eel, the electric catfish, the stargazers, the torpedo rays and finally the skates. In most cases the electric organs are formed from different parts of the body. On the other hand, there is only one way in which a fish can make an electric organ, and that is by a modification and specialisation of the muscle cells and their nerve supply, for it is by this method that all the electric organs of the fish we have examined have been evolved.

The electric organs of the electric eel have proved to be extremely valuable tools in the hands of nerve physiologists. Because they act in the same way as nerves magnified many hundreds of times they have provided information which has eluded workers studying single nerves.

In the past few decades, too, man has been investigating the possibility of using electricity to catch fish himself. After all, it seemed that if the electric eel and the electric catfish could stun or kill other fish by a high-voltage discharge of electricity into the surrounding water then it should be possible to design fishing apparatus based upon the same principle.

It was found that if two metal rods connected to a direct current generator were put into the water, any fish near enough to be affected were drawn towards the positive rod. They behaved as though hypnotised, and were incapable of swimming away. It was then a simple matter to scoop them up in a net. Even the largest and craftiest fish could be enticed from its lair by this modern electronic pied-piper.

From angling by electricity it would seem to be only a step to deep-sea fishing using correspondingly larger apparatus, and some progress has been made with investigations in this direction. Electrical fishing could have important advantages over the present method of trawling. The trawl is an indiscriminate means of catching fish, small as well as large fish being scooped off the sea-bed into the huge net. Although all fish below a certain size are returned to the sea to continue growing, a great many of them have been either killed or too badly injured to survive. Trawling therefore does considerable harm by reducing the potential catch of future years. By contrast, electrical fishing may well lead to controlling the size of the fish attracted to the nets by varying the strength of the electrical discharge. Then only fully-grown fish of marketable size need be caught, and the smaller ones would escape injury.

CHAPTER 12

Protective Coloration and Camouflage

THE ability to change colour so as to blend as closely as possible with its surroundings is a protective device employed by many different kinds of animal. The mechanisms by which animals change their skin colour and pattern in order to become inconspicuous and therefore more difficult for their enemies to find have been the subject of a good deal of investigation.

Some of the most important pioneer work in this interesting field was carried out on the Aesop prawn, *Hipployte varians*, a small prawn about an inch in length. It usually lives in rock pools, attached to the fronds of seaweeds, but it is extremely difficult to locate owing to its outstanding ability to acquire the exact colour of its background. Large numbers of special pigment cells spread over the surface of the body enable it to do this. In the centre of each cell a number of different pigments are concentrated, any one of which can spread out through the cell to colour it. By varying the types and amounts of the pigments distributed, almost any colour can be produced.

Plaice and other flatfish such as the turbot have considerable ability to change both the colour and the pattern of their upper surfaces according to the type of ground on which they are lying. On a gravel bed the skin takes on a much more mottled appearance than when on sand, while yet another pattern is assumed by flatfish living on mud. Many experiments have been conducted with plaice and other flatfish in aquarium tanks with various coloured backgrounds, and every time the fish have proved able to match the unusual background with considerable accuracy in a few seconds. The lower surface of these flatfish, which is hidden from view beneath the animal, develops no pigment and remains white.

Colour change in plaice and other flatfish is achieved by a different method from that so successfully employed by the Aesop prawn. Several types of colour cells are present in the skin, each type having pigment of one particular colour evenly distributed through it. These cells, called chromatophores, are themselves capable of spreading out to expose a large coloured surface, or of contracting to reduce the exposed surface to a mere point. Colours and patterns needed to match

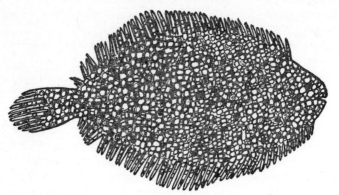

The pattern assumed by a plaice lying on gravel

varying backgrounds are achieved by adjusting the spread of these different chromatophores. The mechanism by which the animal perceives the colour and pattern of the background and then regulates its chromatophores to produce a match is not yet clearly understood. It has been discovered that a blind plaice is unable to make any adjustments to its colour or pattern. It seems, therefore, that the background pattern influences the chromatophore changes through the eyes of the fish and not through direct influence on the chromatophores.

When plaice are kept in experimental tanks illuminated from beneath, the normal colourless under-surfaces of the fish develop chromatophores. This suggests that light may well be the stimulus for normal pigment production in the chromatophores of the upper surface.

When they are not moving about on the sea-bed in search of food, flatfish further camouflage themselves by covering their bodies with a thin layer of sand or mud, leaving little more than their eyes protruding above the surface. To do this they flap their bodies a few times, sending up clouds of sand or mud which then settle on them. They can be seen doing this in an aquarium tank where, in spite of the bright lights, a fish as large as a turbot can make itself almost invisible.

Chamaeleons are perhaps the best known of all the animals which change the colour of their bodies to match their surroundings and thus make themselves inconspicuous to their enemies. In fact, despite its popular reputation, the chamaeleon is not as expert in changing its colour as most of the other animals described in this chapter. Frogs, too, can similarly adopt a wide range of colours to suit their surroundings, from dark brown to light greenish-yellow.

Frogs, chamaeleons and the Aesop prawn all have one characteristic in common. It takes them several hours to adjust their colour to match their surroundings if they have moved from a background of different pattern or colour. The mechanism of colour change is the same in all of them. It is brought about by secretions called hormones produced by special ductless glands. These hormones pass into the blood of the animal and so reach whichever part of the body they are designed to affect.

In contrast the common octopus can change its colour almost instantaneously. Although it terrorises all kinds of animals, it is vulnerable to the cod and the conger eel, and this ability to change colour rapidly as it swims away from its pursuers often enables it to escape. As with other colour-changing animals the common octopus has pigment cells or melanophores widely distributed in its skin. In the octopus, however, these melanophores are not under the control of hormones, but are in direct contact with the nervous system. It is for this reason that colour changes in the common octopus can be effected almost instantaneously. No other kind of animal can change its colour as rapidly as the common octopus and its relatives the squids. The common octopus is said to change colour as its emotions change, and has been observed to flush at the sight of food. In an aquarium tank or a bath it is a fascinating creature to watch as it changes its colour almost continously.

The more active squids and cuttle fish have another extremely ingenious method of eluding their pursuers: laying their own smoke screens. Within the body there is a bag known as the ink-sac, which is filled with an inky fluid. When hard pressed the animal shoots this liquid into the water behind it, where it forms a dense cloud. A rapid change of colour effected by the melanophores, and perhaps a quick change of direction, both serve to increase its chances of escape still further. The 'ink' contained in the ink-sac is the sepia of the artist, and is extracted mainly from *Sepia officinalis*, a cuttle fish common both in British waters and in the Mediterranean, where large numbers are caught for pigment extraction.

An astonishing modification of the smoke-screen theme is exhibited by some of the sea cucumbers. These are among the least known members of the starfish and sea urchin group. The body of a sea cucumber is elongated and worm-like, but it is built on the same radial plan as its better-known relatives. As in the starfish, its skin is toughened by isolated skeletal plates.

Many of the sea cucumbers feed on minute organisms which live in the sea in great abundance, and their method of capturing them is fascinating. They have ten branched tentacles surrounding the mouth, and these are covered with a sticky fluid which traps the organisms.

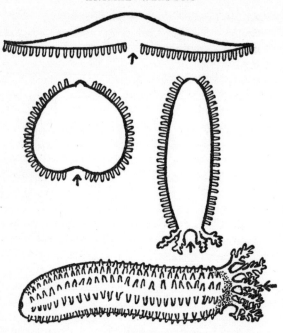

Structural relationships between starfish, sea urchin and sea cucumber.
Above: starfish. Middle left: sea urchin. Middle right: sea cucumber.
Bottom: sea cucumber in its normal position on the sea bed

When a good haul has been achieved the tentacles are curved round itno
the mouth and withdrawn through another special Y-shaped tentacle
which scrapes off the sticky fluid with its trapped food organisms much
as a child might lick jam off its fingers.

Many sea cucumbers when threatened by an attacking enemy cast
out all their internal organs in its face, and in the resulting confusion the
attack is usually broken off. Their powers of regeneration are phenomenal, for in a few days they are able to grow an entirely new set, which
will last until they are next threatened.

One type of sea cucumber, a large dark-brown species known variously as the nigger or cotton spinner, has developed a similar but less
drastic method of dealing with dangerous pursuers. Inside the hind end
of its gut there are some glands called cotton glands. When the animal
is attacked or irritated it can shoot out from these a mass of sticky
threads from which the potential enemy takes some time to untangle
itself. It is in a very real sense 'gummed up', and the sea cucumber is
usually then left alone.

Perhaps the most ingenious methods of camouflage are those adopted by the various species of spider crabs. These crabs are easily recognised by their long thin legs and small triangular bodies. The front of the shell is continued forward as a beak or rostrum. In spite of their long legs spider crabs are very slow and awkward in their movements. In fact to watch one walking gives the impression that every movement is painful.

Although they are quite common, these spider crabs are not easy to find, for their shells are often covered with seaweeds and all sorts of sedentary animals growing on them. Certain sedentary animals, like the acorn barnacles, often make their homes on a spider crab's back, and, whether the crab likes it or not, it has no means of dislodging them except at its annual moult, when it sheds its old shell with everything attached to it and replaces it with a new one. The interesting thing about the excessive plant and animal growth on the spider crab's back is that, far from being unwelcome, it is actually in the main planted there for camouflage by the crab itself. The crab's shell is even provided with hooked hairs to make the attachment of these camouflage organisms easier.

A spider crab shows considerable skill in dressing-up, always attaching plants and animals which blend with its surroundings so as to make it as inconspicuous as possible. If it moves into different surroundings the old camouflage can be removed and replaced by a new set. Once when a specimen wearing various green seaweeds was put into an aquarium tank where the weeds were all red it spent many hours laboriously removing the green weeds one by one and replacing them by red weeds. To enable spider crabs to do this dressing-up their claws are designed to reach every part of the shell, a point to be remembered when handling them.

Encrusting sponges will often be found among the sedentary animals growing on the backs of spider crabs. One crab, the sponge crab, *Dromia vulgaris*, camouflages its shell by covering it completely with the sponge *Ficulina ficus*. *Dromia* is not a spider crab, but is similar in appearance to the edible and shore crabs. It is quite small, seldom exceeding a width of three inches, and is most common in the Mediterranean, though it does sometimes appear on the Cornish coast. In one respect, though, it is specialised. Its last pair of walking legs are turned permanently upwards and are provided with small pincers.

When it is young the sponge crab searches for a small specimen of the sponge. This when found is carefully placed on the top of the shell, which is quite hairy in appearance on account of the large number of

F

hair-like setae covering it. The sponge is held in place by the last pair of upturned walking legs. As the crab grows, so also does the sponge, until it forms a yellow cap fitting right over the shell and concealing the crab beneath. When at rest with its legs and claws tucked away beneath it the crab is invisible to any potential enemy viewing it from above.

The hermit crab is also an expert in the art of camouflage, but its method is different from that of all other crabs. It has lost most of its own armour, except at the front end, and lives for protection with its soft abdomen tucked away in an empty marine snail shell. As it grows, it is always needing more spacious accommodation. House hunting in fact becomes a major obsession, its whole behaviour being centred around this problem.

Its structure is much modified compared with that of an ordinary crab. Both claws remain well armoured, but the right one is much larger than the left. It not only serves as an excellent weapon for attack and defence but is also used as a very effective door to block the entrance when the crab withdraws completely into its borrowed shell.

The first two pairs of walking legs are well developed, and enable it to run about on the sea-bed or along the floor of a rock pool carrying its home on its back. But the last two pairs are quite small and never come out of the shell. All the armour has gone from the abdomen, which is permanently twisted so as to fit into the coils of the shell, and the swimmerets are reduced to a few hairy wisps, which are still used by the female for attaching the eggs during the breeding season. Only the last pair are at all well developed, and these have become modified to form a pair of sickle-shaped hooks.

If you pick up a hermit crab from a rock pool to have a closer look at it, you will feel a jerk and probably hear a sharp click as it suddenly withdraws into its shell. By persuading a hermit crab to forsake its own house and take over a glass model it has been possible to see exactly what goes on inside the shell. The sickle-shaped hooks are used to anchor the abdomen to the central pillar of the shell. When anything moves in front of it, this grip is tightened and the last two short pairs of walking legs stiffen and brace the body against the shell. These precautionary measures enable the crab to resist any attempts to pull it out of its shell. In fact you cannot dislodge a hermit crab without seriously injuring it.

When the crab suddenly withdraws into its shell, it does so by flexing its abdomen – the same muscular movement which shoots a lobster or a prawn backwards through the water. In a rough sea the crab withdraws into its shell so that it can be rolled about by the waves without suffering damage.

From the time of its last larval moult the hermit crab's housing problems begin. A very tiny shell suffices at first, but the small crab is growing rapidly and undergoing frequent moults, each necessitating a new and slightly larger house.

The hermit crab is an amusing little creature in an aquarium where its antics can be watched and its house-hunting habits studied. When it needs a new home it usually examines many shells, probing into each carefully with its claws to make sure that it is empty and clean, before at last deciding on the one which suits it. Then it removes its abdomen from the old shell and thrusts it quickly into the new one, as though it realises the danger of leaving this unarmoured part of its body exposed for longer than is necessary. Even when quite suited for the time being the house hunting instinct is so strong that no hermit crab seems able to resist examining every empty shell it comes across.

With its unprotected abdomen safely tucked away within the coils of a suitable shell the hermit crab is exceedingly pugnacious, always ready to fight with its fellows. Sometimes there is a fierce struggle between two crabs for the possession of the same new house, or one crab will try to dislodge the other from the one it has. If the occupying crab has been foolish enough to take a shell which is rather too big for it, it will probably be ejected, but if its shell fits properly it will usually be able to retain it against all attacks.

Camouflage is generally used as a protective device, to make the animal adopting it more difficult for its enemies to find. There is, however, a group of spiders known as crab spiders which employ camouflage in order to make themselves inconspicuous to their potential victims, who therefore come close enough to be caught without realising the presence of their predators. This is known as aggressive camouflage. Their group name refers to the fact that they can move sideways just as readily as they can move forwards or backwards, since typical crabs are noted for their sideways movements.

There are three main groups of crab spiders classified not by any anatomical characteristics but by their behaviour. Members of the first group variously resemble pieces of dead leaf or the bark of trees, the former living on the ground and the latter on tree-trunks and branches. In both cases the crab spiders simply lie perfectly still until a suitable unsuspecting insect victim passes close enough to be pounced upon and caught.

The second and perhaps the best known group of crab spiders lives in flowers. They are often in fact referred to as flower spiders. They are brightly coloured, and lurk in flowers which have the same colour as themselves. It is virtually impossible to detect them, and the same is obviously true of the insects upon which they prey. They will remain in their flowers if necessary for hours on end without making the slightest movement. Removed from their flowers they are seen to be extremely beautiful.

At least one species of crab spider, *Misumena vatia*, is able to change colour, which gives it a wider choice of flowers in which it can be inconspicuous. It changes from white to yellow by transferring a yellow pigment from its intestine to its skin, and so can lurk unnoticed in a yellow flower. If it then decides to take up residence in a white flower it simply reabsorbs the yellow pigment.

The third group of crab spiders is perhaps the most ingenious of them all. These spiders resemble bird droppings, not, you would think, a very profitable subject for imitation. Butterflies, however, are attracted to bird droppings because they contain moisture and mineral salts which they need. Accordingly butterflies approach these disguised spiders as they would genuine bird droppings, and are pounced upon as soon as they settle.

Their resemblance to bird droppings probably serves another purpose: protecting them from their own potential enemies. Certainly quite a number of different species of moths have derived benefit from camouflaging themselves so that they look like bird droppings. They adopt this pose during the daytime when they are resting on leaves. A more efficient method of protection against birds, which are their main enemies, can hardly be imagined.

Returning to aggressive camouflage, perhaps the best known exponents are the praying mantids. All of them have the gift of complete patience, which enables them to remain perfectly still on the twig they have chosen as their hunting post. Many of them in addition are so coloured as to blend completely with their immediate surroundings. Thus their victims approach without fear or awareness of their presence. Their camouflage is defensive as well as aggressive, because they have no other protection against insect-eating birds and lizards, for which they are desirable prey.

Mantids are relatives of the cockroaches whose first pair of legs are extremely well developed as weapons. The tibia and femur are both covered with powerful spines, and can be snapped back on each other to trap their prey like the two blades of a pair of scissors, an operation which can be completed in less than one-tenth of a second. The most sophisticated species are those which have come to resemble flowers so closely that it is virtually impossible to distinguish them when they are sitting among the flowers they are imitating. One of the first of these flower simulators to be discovered was the rose-leaf mantis of southern India, aptly described by the late Dr J. Anderson, who made a close study of its habits.

On looking at the insects from above they do not exhibit any very striking features beyond the leaf-like expansion of the prothorax and the foliaceous appendages of the limbs, both of which, like the upper surface of the insect, are coloured green, but on turning to the under surface the aspect is entirely different. The leaf-like expansion of the prothorax, instead of being green, is a clear, pale lavender-violet, with a faint pink bloom along the edges, so that this portion has the exact apparance of the corolla of a plant, a floral simulation which is perfected by the presence of a dark, blackish-brown dot in the centre, over the prothorax, and which mimics the opening of the tube of a corolla. A favourite position of the insect is to hang head downwards among a mass of green foliage and, when it does this, it generally remains motionless, but, at intervals, evinces a swaying movement as of a flower touched by a gentle breeze; and while in this attitude, with its fore-limbs banded violet and black, and drawn up in front of the centre of the corolla, the simulation of a papilionaceous flower is complete. The object of the bright colouring of the under-surface of the prothorax is evident, its purpose being to act as a decoy to insects, which, mistaking it for a corolla, fly directly into the expectant, sabre-like arms of the simulator.

Another important type of camouflage is the adoption of a white coat by mammals which live among snow. Perhaps the best known of the permanently white animals is the polar bear which, if it remains perfectly still, can be approached quite closely without being detected, which means that its potential victims can also come within the danger distance without being aware of any danger.

More interesting than the permanently white animals are those which with the onset of winter change their coat from brown or grey to white. Two examples may be mentioned. In the British Isles there are several different species of hares. One of these, the Scottish blue hare, lives in the mountains of Scotland where it will be surrounded with snow during the winter months. Accordingly it replaces its normal summer coat with white fur for the winter, the change occurring at the autumn moult which is undergone by the vast majority of mammals. The summer coat has a general bluish-grey appearance, though there is also some brown in it.

The stoat is another mammal which can change its normal brown coat for a white coat at the onset of winter. The stoat is about fourteen inches in length with a characteristic black tip to its tail, which distinguishes it from its somewhat smaller relative, the weasel. It moults twice a year, and sometimes the winter coat is white, except for the black tip to the tail. The white coat of the stoat is known as ermine. Whether a stoat has a white winter coat seems to depend mainly upon latitude or temperature. In the far north of Britain every stoat changes colour, whereas in the south of England white stoats are a rarity. In Scotland the majority change colour. In Britain the weasel never has a white winter coat, but in northern Europe white weasels are fairly common in winter.

Several different kinds of insects have perfected methods of camouflaging their bodies by various exudations from their own glands. But before we consider these we should look at the larvae of certain lacewings, which hide their bodies beneath an accumulation of debris. Lacewings belong to the insect order Neuroptera, which also includes the alder flies and the snake flies. They all have two pairs of gauzy wings which close like a roof over their bodies. Lacewings are common in gardens in the summer, and tend to come indoors in the autumn to hibernate. Many of them are green in colour.

Some of the lacewings have larvae which are broad and short, and these bear all over their dorsal surfaces small hooked bristles. In order to hide themselves they deliberately seize materials in their mandibles and place them on their backs by bending their heads backwards where they are firmly fixed by the hooked bristles. The materials they use for this ingenious covering are the dry husks of their victims' bodies and small pieces of dry plant material. Once they are completely covered they are virtually undetectable by their potential enemies.

The frog-hoppers or cuckoo-spit insects have achieved a high degree of success in camouflaging their bodies with their own exudations. They belong to the insect order Hemiptera, which also includes the aphids and the scale insects. Our other two examples of self camouflage in fact come one from each of these two groups. The frog-hoppers owe their common name partly to their frog-like appearance and partly to the ability of the adults to leap considerable distances if threatened or touched. The Hemiptera are one of the orders of insects in which there are usually no separate larval or caterpillar and pupal or chrysalis stages, the egg developing into a nymph which progresses directly through a series of moults and growth stages to become an adult.

Frog-hopper nymphs live, as do many other members of the order, by sucking plant juices. The froth with which they surround and hide themselves is produced from a mixture of sugary sap, wax and digestive juices whipped up into a kind of lather by blowing air through it. Although the cuckoo-spit itself is so obvious, the tiny nymph within it is of course completely hidden from the view of its enemies. Sir J. Arthur Thomson said very aptly that the frog-hopper's nymph contrives to 'live under water and yet in the air, conspicuous and yet concealed, in the sunshine and yet cool'.

The woolly aphid or American blight, *Eriosoma lanigerum*, is a well-known pest of apple trees in many parts of the world. The 'cotton wool' with which it covers its colonies is a waxy edudation from the creature's skin, and serves to give it a protective covering. As with the frog-hopper nymph, its covering may be extremely conspicuous, but the animal itself is hidden from its enemies.

Perhaps the most interesting of all the methods of camouflage with products originating from the body of the animal itself is the covering produced by an Indian scale insect, the lac insect *Tachardia lacca*. The name lac, or lakh, means a hundred thousand, and refers to the vast numbers in which these tiny insects occur. It is found on nearly a hundred different trees, most of them belonging to the genus *Ficus*. The young insects puncture the trees with their piercing mouth parts and suck up the sap. They then exude from their bodies a resinous secretion which covers and protects their bodies. So dense are they, and so much secretion does each one produce, that the twigs on which they are living become covered with a layer so thick that it can be removed and used commercially.

The twigs are known as stick lac, and the encrusting layers can be melted off. They form the shellac of commerce, used in the manufacture of varnish, gramophone records and sealing wax. The red colouring matter which it contains can be separated out as a pigment or dye. This is the original crimson lake formerly used by the artist until it was replaced by the modern manufactured aniline dye equivalent.

One of the most ingenious methods of deception for protection is practised by certain insects whose hind ends have come to resemble their heads, presumably causing predators to attack the relatively unimportant hind end, thus enabling the rest of the insect, including the head, to escape.

Butterflies of the genus *Thecla* bear antenna-like appendages at the hind ends of their wings, and attention is drawn to these deceptive outgrowths by a convergence of stripes on the wings. The idea that the purpose of this resemblance is deception is reinforced by the fact that when these butterflies land they swing rapidly round to face the opposite

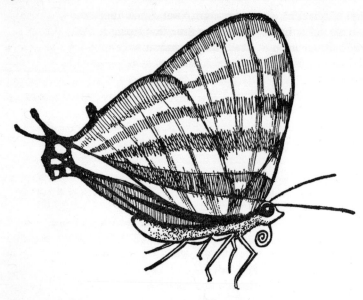

The antenna-like appendages on the hind ends of the wings of the
tropical butterfly *Thecla* (left) distract attention from the inconspicuous
real head end

way, and if attacked they fly off in this direction. A butterfly landing on
a vertical surface almost invariably rests with its head end uppermost,
but these species settle with the head pointing downwards, thus again
tempting any predator to attack the relatively unimportant hind end.
Even if such an attack results in the loss of a considerable proportion of
the hind end of the wings, this is not very serious, for the normal wing
area of a butterfly is much greater than it really needs to fly.

Another particularly convincing example of the head-tail deception
is shown by the lantern fly from Thailand. The hind ends of the wings
have become modified to resemble prominent antennae, a black beak
and well-developed eyes. The true head is in fact much smaller and is
held close to the ground, in which position it would in any case be
inconspicuous.

Many snakes adopt a similar technique by moving their tails, often
brightly coloured, while keeping their true heads completely still and
close to the ground.

Some animals which are not sufficiently active to escape from their
enemies by fleeing gain protection by feigning death. Many weevils, for
example, instantly draw in their legs and antennae when alarmed and

fall to the ground, where they are almost impossible to detect since they resemble small lumps of soil. Pill beetles are even more skilled in the art of appearing dead. They can fold themselves up like a penknife at the first hint of danger. The head is retracted into the thorax and the antennae are closely folded against its sides. The joints of the legs are doubled back on one another, and each folded leg fits into a groove on

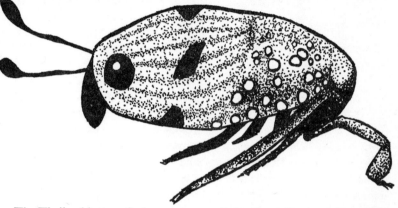

The Thailand lantern fly has a most convincing bogus head at its hind end (left), the real head end being relatively inconspicuous

the underside of the thorax. The result of these efforts is that the beetle looks like a small round stone which even if handled betrays not the slightest sign of life. It is difficult to imagine any potential predator taking an interest in what to it must appear to be an inanimate object.

The ability to leap or jump suddenly is another valuable method used by some insects to escape from their enemies. Grasshoppers, for example, are great and powerful jumpers, and because of this they are difficult for their potential enemies to catch. Grasshoppers jump by means of their extremely powerful third pair of legs, so that their leaps are brought about in a manner similar to that of a kangaroo. Click-beetles, or skipjacks as they are commonly called, use quite a different method to produce an equally effective jump. If a click-beetle is touched or in any other way alarmed it curls up its legs and drops to the ground as effectively as if it had been shot, and lies for a few seconds as still as death, with its body curled up. Then suddenly the body is straightened, and the beetle is jerked into the air for a distance of several inches. Until it is satisfied that danger has passed it will continue to repeat these aerial jumps.

An instructive example of the part which camouflage can play in evolution is shown by the recent history of the peppered moth, *Biston betularia*. Until the middle of the last century this would have been described as a light coloured moth with white wings speckled with black – hence the name peppered. In about 1850, however, a single black specimen was found in Manchester. Despite its unusual colouring entomologists had no difficulty in identifying it as a specimen of *Biston*.

From this time on the black variety became steadily more common in towns, though remaining virtually unknown in the country. By 1900 it had become the dominant variety in Manchester, only one in a hundred being of the normal light colour, and the position was similar in other large industrial towns.

This march of the dark variety of the peppered moth closely paralleled and followed the development of heavy industry after the Industrial Revolution. The increasing volume of smoke from factory and domestic chimneys stained black the bark of trees as well as everything else. Tree bark, usually lichen covered, is light in colour, and a normal peppered moth settling on such a branch or trunk would be inconspicuous, but on blackened bark where the lichen had been killed, it would be extremely easy to see and an easy victim for insectivorous birds. The newly emerging dark variety, however, would be extremely well camouflaged on the blackened bark, and conversely very conspicuous on bark of normal colour.

These, then, are the facts, but what of the explanation? What biological process has brought about the colour divisions in a species which had hitherto been uniform? There were two possible theories to consider. One of these postulated that the caterpillars living on the smoke-contaminated leaves absorbed the soot with their food, and that this caused them eventually to produce black moths. Despite much experimental work, no evidence emerged to prove that black food could induce the production of black adult moths.

The alternative theory postulated that the black form of the moth had always existed, but had never multiplied because it was so conspicuous that it was soon killed and eaten by insectivorous birds. The changed conditions brought about by industrialisation, however, would for the first time provide an environment which favoured the black variety. As a result the black individuals would live longer than the normal peppered ones, and would therefore leave more offspring. As this process went on, so the proportion of black moths would increase steadily until they formed a substantial majority. If this proved to be true it would be an interesting example of evolution by natural selection such as Charles Darwin had postulated.

Dr H. B. D. Kettlewell has carried out a very thorough programme of research which has shown the second theory to be the correct one. By breeding extensively from normal peppered moths he has been able to show that small numbers of the black variety are produced, and that in fact black is genetically a dominant factor.

He also released groups of moths containing equal numbers of the two varieties both in country and heavily industrialised areas. The moths were all marked with coloured dots on the under sides of the wings, and each night a mercury vapour lamp trap was placed in the area in which they had been released. Each night the proportion of black moths recovered in the rural areas became less and less, showing that they were being eliminated at a faster rate than the normal coloured moths. But in the industrial areas the findings were exactly reversed, the proportion of normal coloured moths recovered becoming less and less, showing that they were being eliminated faster than the black variety.

CHAPTER 13

Warning Coloration and Mimicry

THE previous chapter described animals which use considerable in-genuity to make themselves as inconspicuous as possible, and so escape the attentions of their enemies. By contrast, the animals we shall look at in this chapter might be assumed to have gone out of their way to make themselves as conspicuous as possible, for they are brightly coloured and boldly patterned, and certainly as successful at surviving as the most perfectly camouflaged species.

In the majority of these brightly coloured species the colours are designed to warn would-be predators that any attempts to eat them would for various reasons be inadvisable. They make no effort to hide from predators; in fact most seem intent on drawing attention to them-selves. Consider for example the wasp. Any bird or lizard (with the exception of bee-eaters, which are apparently immune to bee and other insect stings), once it has made the mistake of taking a wasp, will never again be tempted to repeat the painful experiment, and by its distinctive appearance the wasp helps to ensure that it is easily recognised. If the wasp's colouring was less brilliant, an individual bird might take several experiences to learn what a wasp looked like.

Of course any species which adopts warning coloration as a defensive mechanism will lose a proportion of its numbers in the interests of education. Each insect-eating bird must learn for itself what happens when a wasp is taken, but the sacrifice of one wasp will ensure immunity from attack by this particular bird for all other wasps. Black and yellow are common warning colours among wasps, and this combination is adopted by many other insects as well, often for rather different reasons which we shall be examining later. Bees are protected in the same way by their type of coloration.

Not all warning colours indicate the possession of stings, however. The red-and-black larvae of the cinnabar moth, and the larvae of the large cabbage white butterfly, conspicuously marked with black spots on a greenish or yellowish ground, make no attempt to hide away on the ragwort plants and the cabbages on which respectively they live, yet they seem effectively to avoid the attentions of insect-eating birds. The reason cannot be that they possess a sting or any similar defensive weapon. They owe their immunity to the fact that birds find them extremely distasteful. Again, as with the wasps, a certain number of individuals have to be eaten to educate each generation of birds.

Many other insects with conspicuous colouring also have an unpleasant taste, among them the larvae of the magpie moth and various saw-flies, as well as the attractive little red ladybirds with their varying numbers of black spots. Magpie-moth caterpillars have been used in a number of experiments designed to prove that conspicuous insects really are avoided. When offered to insectivorous birds, lizards, frogs and even bats they were almost always refused, being either rejected on sight or dropped as soon as they were taken into the mouth. Young chickens which had never seen magpie larvae before attempted to eat them, but dropped them without swallowing them. After a few experiences they refused to have anything more to do with them.

Many other experiments have provided overwhelming evidence of the efficacy of warning coloration to those insects possessing it. A Dutch naturalist, I. H. N. Kluijver, carried out an extended study over a three-year period of the food which the parents provided for nestling starlings. No fewer than 16,484 insects were logged. Among these there were 4,490 beetles, but only two of them were ladybirds. This must have been the result of deliberate selection by the parent birds because there was no shortage of ladybirds in the vicinity of the nests. Of 799 *Hymenoptera* brought to the nests there was not a single wasp or bee, and again wasps and bees were both very plentiful in the neighbourhood.

H. B. Cott carried out a similar investigation in East Africa and in the Canary Islands of the insects found in the stomachs of 995 frogs. Of 11,585 insects recovered only twenty had warning-type coloration, though in both areas insects with warning coloration were both conspicuous and plentiful.

Besides colour, attitudes also can be used as warnings. The devil's coach-horse, *Staphylinus olens*, one of the rove beetles, adopts a threatening stance when alarmed or threatened. It curves its abdomen over its back and holds its mandibles wide apart, snapping vigorously at whatever threatens it, At the same time it exudes an unpleasant liquid from glands at the end of the abdomen. This threatening attitude is more than just bluff, for the beetle will press home its attack with its formidable jaws. The earwig behaves similarly, brandishing its forceps above its head, quite ready to use them if pressed. Of all such insects the most frightening must be the male stag beetle, *Lucanus cervus*, with its pair of large mandibles held wide apart. In this case the attitude is mainly bluff, because these impressive-looking mandibles are capable of only a feeble bite. The female beetle, although its mandibles are much smaller and less impressive, is capable of inflicting a much more effective nip.

One of the most formidable of all animal threats, because of the potentially fatal consequences of ignoring it, is the warning display of the cobra as it raises its body vertically from the ground and spreads it hood, accompanying the visible threat with an audible hiss. Contrary to popular opinion, the cobra does not really want a full confrontation. It hopes that the warning will be heeded and that it will be left to go its own way. Similarly, the rattle of the rattlesnake is an audible warning that it does not wish to be disturbed, and one which it is clearly in any other animal's best interests to heed. The warning of these snakes is given in the same spirit as 'We do not want to fight, but by jingo if we do . . .', for they certainly have the armament to back up their threats.

Even frogs use warning coloration. Certain South American species belonging to the genus *Dendrobates* produce a secretion from the skin poisonous enough to kill any small animal which attempts to eat them. In fact the native populations have always used this poison as the dressing for their poisoned arrows, and minute amounts on the tips of the arrows can prove fatal to their human adversaries. These frogs are all brightly, even luridly, coloured in black and red or black and yellow.

One of the most universal protective devices in the animal kingdom is the eyespot, a coloured part of the body so fashioned as to resemble a staring eye. The effect on other animals is almost always to scare them and deter them from attacking. Most animals which use this particularly effective device are bluffing and lack any means of defence if their bluff is called.

Among the most familiar of all the specialists in the production of eyespots are butterflies and moths, and of these the peacock butterfly has been the subject of much investigation. In the resting position, with the wings folded together above the body, the peacock butterfly is extremely well camouflaged, being difficult to detect against a typical background. But if it suddenly flaps its wings it reveals a completely different, brightly coloured and startling appearance, sufficient to cause a bird to abandon any designs it may have had on the resting butterfly. Tests with birds have indeed shown that the sudden revelation of the peacock butterfly's eyes does have the effect of scaring them. That it really is the eyes which deter has been proved by brushing off the scales which form the eyes and then offering the butterflies to birds. In the absence of the eyes the birds show no signs of being frightened of the butterflies, catching them without hesitation.

The eyes of the peacock butterfly cannot be classified as warning coloration, because the butterfly is neither dangerous nor unpleasant for the birds to eat. It is purely a bluffing device, but an extremely successful one.

The eyed hawk moth uses a similar device. At rest on the trunk of a tree, with its camouflaged forewings covering its hind wings, it is very difficult to detect. But if it is disturbed it moves its forewings forward to uncover the hind wings, on each of which is a prominent eyespot. Experimental investigation has shown that the sudden revelation of these eyespots has precisely the same deterrent effect on birds as the disclosure of the eyespots on the wings of the peacock butterfly. Again the eyespots are being used as bluff, for the eyed hawk moth is just as palatable to birds as the peacock butterfly.

The caterpillar of the elephant hawk moth has developed a particularly effective variation on the eyespot theme. When undisturbed among the leaves of its food plants it is quite effectively concealed by its general brown colour. But if it is disturbed or alarmed it suddenly withdraws its head and the three following segments into those behind them. As a result the whole front end of the body swells out to resemble the front end of some animal with four very large eye-like structures. Birds in captivity have been shown to exhibit alarm when these displaying caterpillars have been shown to them, and they will not approach their seed bowl if one of them is placed in it.

Darwin suggested that the much smaller eyespots on the wings of many butterflies may protect their owners in a different way: that these small eyes on the wings might focus the attention of a bird or a lizard so that it struck at them, thus removing part of the wing but allowing the butterfly itself to escape. As we saw in chapter 12, since butterfly wings have a much greater area than is really necessary for the insect's rather weak and erratic flight it suffers little by this partial loss.

The spectacular tails of the swallowtail butterflies may possibly serve the same protective purpose, distracting the attention of the pursuing bird so that it snaps at the tail, which is of no essential value to the butterfly, thus allowing it to escape.

Certain South American beetles have eyespots on their hard integument, and presumably these serve the same purpose as the eyespots on butterflies and moths. Another tropical American insect, the so-called alligator bug, has a strange hollow projection from the front of its head. Seen from the side, this resembles a miniature alligator's head, complete with representations of the alligator's eyes, nostrils and formidable rows of teeth, and with a dark line giving the impression of jaws slightly opened. As Julian Huxley has put it, 'a bird or a little monkey picking over the foliage and coming suddenly upon what looks like a grinning and repulsive reptilian head would scarcely be encouraged to continue its explorations'.

It is now time to turn our attention to the remarkable phenomenon of mimicry, a phenomenon first brought to the attention of the scientific world by a famous nineteenth-century English naturalist Henry W. Bates. For eleven years, from 1849 until 1860, Bates wandered through the Brazilian forests observing and collecting, fascinated especially by the butterflies of the region.

Having assembled representative collections of two quite distinct families, the whites (family *Pieridae*) and the heliconids (family *Heliconiidae*), Bates' attention was drawn to the appearance of certain of the white species. Normally the whites have white wings, as their name suggests, whereas the heliconids are brightly coloured. But in his collection there were some white species which instead of white wings had coloured wings. Even more remarkable was the fact that these unusual-coloured species all differed from one another, but each one bore an extremely close resemblance both in colour and in pattern to one of the heliconid species.

Bates argued that if pierids had come to resemble certain heliconids they must derive some advantage from the resemblance. In the area in which he had collected his butterflies he recorded that heliconids were both abundant and conspicuous, and furthermore flew so slowly that they would be extremely easy for birds to catch. Insectivorous birds were also plentiful in the area, but apparently the birds ignored the butterflies. The only possible explanation was that the butterflies were unpalatable to the birds. Assuming that he had his facts right, Bates argued that the pierid butterflies which had made themselves almost indistinguishable from the heliconids were probably edible butterflies which hoped to escape being eaten by birds by looking like inedible butterflies.

Bates' work led to the idea of a palatable insect miming an unpalatable one by becoming in external appearance almost indistinguishable from it, and so gaining protection from its enemies under false pretences. The phenomenon thus became known as mimicry, and this particular type of mimicry – because, as we shall see, there is another type – is universally referred to as Batesian mimicry in acknowledgement of Henry Bates' pioneer work. If Batesian mimicry is to be effective it seems necessary for the model, that is the animal which is avoided for some good reason, to be more common than the mimic, the harmless animal which is gaining protection.

Wasps and bees, as we have already seen, indulge in warning coloration which effectively deters potential predators from attacking them. An amazing number of other insects from several different orders mimic various wasps and bees and apparently as a result achieve quite a high degree of immunity from birds, reptiles and other animals to which they would in fact be palatable. Hover-flies are particularly noted for their ability to mimic, some species having modified their colouring so as to look remarkably like wasps, while others, notably the common drone fly, have come to be virtually indistinguishable from bees. One inter-

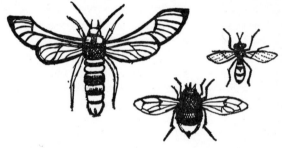

Insects resembling bees and wasps: hornet clearwing moth (left), which gains protection by its resemblance to the hornet. Hover fly resembling a bee (centre) harmless hover fly resembling a wasp (right)

esting fact about these flies is that as members of the order Diptera they have but a single pair of wings, whereas the true wasps and bees, belonging to the order Hymenoptera, have two pairs of wings. This difference, though, is virtually unnoticeable, body colouring being the all-important factor in producing effective mimicry. There is even a species of beetle, the wasp beetle, which has developed a typical yellow-and-black striped body to produce a passable imitation of a wasp.

Moths, with their opaque wings covered with scales, might seem to be the last insects capable of mimicking wasps and bees. And yet a few species have done so very successfully. The hornet clearwing and the lunar hornet clearwing have transparent wings and banded wasp-like bodies which give them a remarkable resemblance to the protected insects they have chosen to mimic. The bee hawk moth also has clear wings, and a furry body reminiscent both in shape and colouring of a typical bee.

Subsequent to Bates' work other naturalists pursued these fascinating studies into the phenomenon of mimicry, and it was not long before another type of mimicry was recognised. Bates himself had been puzzled by the fact that certain unrelated species of butterflies were virtually identical in appearance and likewise unpalatable to birds. These examples clearly did not fit into his scheme of mimicry. The explanation was left to Fritz Müller, a German zoologist who also spent a good deal of time doing field work in Brazil. In 1879 he put forward his theory that such resemblances between two unpalatable species represented a different kind of mimicry. If two species could be recognised as one by their potential enemies, each of them would have to sacrifice a smaller number of individuals to educate each year's young birds, because catching only one insect would teach each bird to avoid members of both species in future. This type of mimicry, by which two or more distasteful species reduce their individual losses by coming to resemble each other, is known as Müllerian mimicry.

Both types of mimicry rely upon the fact that individual birds, or indeed any other animals, really are capable of learning from unpleasant experiences, so that if they take an unpalatable insect once they will not do so again. Today a great deal of experimental evidence supports the theories of Bates and Müller.

In 1960 Jean Brower published the results of a series of experiments on butterfly mimics and models using a species of American jay as her experimental predator. She used two species of butterflies belonging to two different families, which were therefore not at all closely related, but were remarkably similar in external appearance. One of these, *Danaus plexippus*, was the unpalatable model, and *Limenitis archippus* the tasty mimic. The birds were first offered *Limenitis*, which they ate without hesitation. They were then offered a number of *Danaus*. Each bird took the first one offered without hesitation, but reacted strongly after biting it and discarded it. A half-hearted attempt might be made to bite the second one offered, and even perhaps the third, but after this these butterflies evoked no response at all. Having thus learned to avoid the impalatable *Danaus* they were once again offered specimens of the palatable *Limenitis*, which before their experiences with *Danaus* they had taken readily. Now, however, they ignored these completely. Similar results were obtained using two other pairs of models and mimics.

In 1965 Jean Brower carried out another series of experiments using the toad *Bufo terrestris*. In the first she used a bumble bee *Bombus americanorum*, which of course has a sting, and the harmless bee robber fly *Mallophora bomboides*, which mimics it. The toads soon learnt to avoid the bumble bees, and from then on they would have nothing to do with the robber flies, although these would have been quite palatable to them. Similar results were obtained in experiments using the common honey bee *Apis mellifica* as the armed model and the hover-fly *Eristalis vinetorum* as the harmless mimic. Even after a lapse of three months many of the toads still avoided bees offered to them. Bees which had had their stings removed were eaten without hesitation, demonstrating that it really was the sting of the bee which established the immunity of both the bees and their mimics.

In further experiments Jean Brower attempted to exclude all possibility of previous knowledge influencing choice by offering artificially coloured mealworms to starlings. First the starlings were fed with normal mealworms which had two segments coloured organge. Other mealworms were made distasteful by dipping them in quinine, and the same two segments were coloured green. Within a very short time all the birds learnt to avoid all mealworms coloured green, even those which had not in fact been dipped in quinine and were therefore quite palatable. They were even avoided when only 40 per cent of them had been treated with quinine, which provided good evidence that mimicry can be effective even though the number of palatable mimics exceeds the number of impalatable models.

Mimicry need not necessarily be confined to colour and pattern. It is possible for a defenceless animal to obtain protection by mimicking the behaviour of a model which is well able to defend itself. Many harmless snakes, for example, will hiss and even go through the motions of striking at an attacker, although their efforts are pure bluff, since they have no venom to back up their threats.

One of the most accomplished of these snake mimics is the North American hog-nosed snake, *Heterodon contortrix*. If disturbed it fills its lungs and hisses, and at the same time flattens its head and neck region by moving its anterior ribs, the same mechanism used by the cobra to spread its hood. If these warnings are not heeded it will raise its head and strike, but if it is watched closely it will be seen that it does not open its mouth. This rather elaborate bluff is only one of the hog-nosed snake's defence mechanisms. If this fails and someone goes to pick it up it will try out its very convincing death feigning act. All its fury seems to disappear and it rolls over on its back and lies limply with its mouth open and its tongue hanging out.

One of the most fascinating of all examples in which an animal of one group mimics one of a completely different and totally unrelated group comes from Malaya. The larva of a small hawk moth, *Panacra mydon*, is normally quite undistinguished as it moves around feeding on leaves, but if it is disturbed and feels itself threatened a complete transformation is effected. The head and first few segments are withdrawn into the segments behind, and these are distended so as to become broad and flat. A pair of eyespots on one of these segments are normally not very realistic, but now they become large and conspicuous. All the abdominal feet except the last two pairs are also retracted, so that the front part of the body now appears cylindrical and legless with a wide 'head', and bears an uncanny resemblance to the head and front part of the body of a small snake. To make the mimicry even more realistic the front part of the body is arched to give it a threatening attitude. Any small lizard or bird confronted with this extremely realistic mimic of a snake is almost certain to leave it severely alone.

Perhaps the most remarkable example of this particular type of mimicry is the hawk moth larva which does not merely appear to be like a small snake, but is in fact like the young of a particular species of Malayan snake, Wagler's pit viper, a common poisonous snake inhabiting the same areas as the hawk moth. When the pit viper grows to full size it changes its colour and pattern completely, so that the caterpillar no longer bears the slightest resemblance to it. Because of the difference in size there would be no point in the caterpillar being like the adult snake.

CHAPTER 14

Animal Partners

MOST animals have no friends, only rivals and enemies, but some do have the companionship and occasional help of other animals of their own kind. A few, however, have learned to cooperate with animals of other kinds so that both creatures benefit from the association. Each helps the other in its struggle for existence, offering or receiving protection in return for help in finding food. These partnerships between species which are often not even remotely related are not common, but they form an interesting and unusual chapter of natural history. Much more common are associations in which one species is living at the expense of the other as a parasite, usually causing it some harm and often ultimate death.

In an ideal partnership both animals derive equal benefit, but there are many examples in which one partner appears to benefit much more than the other. Indeed in some cases the advantage seems to be entirely with one partner, but it is always possible that the other partner may derive some advantage which we know nothing about.

There are really two different kinds of partnerships between different species of animals. The first is external, in which the partners are free to leave each other's company and lead independent lives if they wish. This is known as commensalism. Then there is symbiosis, which is a more complete kind of association in which one species lives right inside the body and tissues of the other, unable to leave its partner even if it wanted to. A few examples of commensalism have already been discussed in previous chapters.

The first suggestion that animals might go into partnership was made by the Greek historian Herodotus. About 2,500 years ago he described how a small bird called the courser came to the assistance of the Nile crocodiles. 'Living in the river,' he wrote, 'the crocodile gets its mouth full of leeches, and when it comes out and opens its jaws to the westerly breezes, the courser goes in and gobbles up the leeches, which good office so pleases the crocodile that it does the courser no harm.'

This seemed to people who read it a very tall story. In fact they found the whole idea that animals might cooperate with one another difficult to believe. Nevertheless it was eventually proved that this little bird, a relative of the plover, does indeed walk up to crocodiles as they bask in the sunshine on the banks of the Nile and pick out the leeches which have collected between their teeth.

The courser is not the only bird which helps crocodiles in this way. The spur-winged lapwing walks right inside the crocodile's mouth to hunt the leeches. While it is inside the crocodile is said to close its jaws, opening them again a few minutes later to let it walk out. These birds

Coursers around a nile crocodile, whose mouth they will rid of parasites

must be very brave to walk into the crocodile's mouth, but the reptile seems to know that they are helping it, for it never attempts to harm them. The advantage to the birds is that they obtain a readily available supply of highly nutritious food.

Another well-known bird partner is the buff-backed heron, more commonly known as the cattle egret. This is a white bird, smaller than the British heron, with long buff plumes sweeping back from the top of the head. It is quite common in many parts of Africa. Cattle egrets are seldom found on their own. They are nearly always in the company of herds of domestic cattle, antelopes, buffalo, hippopotamuses and other grazing animals. As these animals eat their way slowly through the grass the egrets show constant activity, running around their legs and diving into the grass, apparently not in the least bit worried about the danger of being trodden on.

If we could get close enough we should see that as the larger animals move through the grass they disturb many grasshoppers, which fly a few yards before disappearing into the grass again. These grasshoppers are the egrets' favourite food, but they are so well camouflaged that it is almost impossible for the birds to see them in the grass. Only when they are disturbed and take to the wing can the birds catch them. If the birds had to rely for their food on the insects they were able to find for themselves they would get little to eat; by disturbing the grasshoppers, the large mammals provide their attendant birds with food in plenty. The various grazing animals have thus become indispensable to the egrets.

But it is not a one-sided arrangement. While some of the birds are running round the feet of the grazing animals, others can be seen walking all over their backs, and pecking at their coats. They are not, however, attacking the cattle, but picking out and eating the many ticks that attack all domestic and wild grazing animals in Africa.

Certain other birds, like the bee-eaters, for example, have also learned that grazing cattle and antelopes disturb insects lying in the grass, but they take advantage of it without doing anything for the cattle in return.

How did this association between the cattle egrets and the various grazing animals first develop? To begin with, the birds probably discovered that these animals disturbed insects as they moved through the grass, and merely took advantage of it, just as the bee-eaters do today. Only much later, perhaps, did they discover the ticks in the animals' hides, and find that they, too, were good to eat. We must imagine then that over the course of a great many years the casual association with cattle became more common, until finally it developed into a habit inherited by every member of the species.

Another African bird, the ox-pecker or tick-bird, has developed an even closer partnership with all kinds of wild grazing animals. It has become modified in structure and behaviour to fit it more efficiently for its life of cooperation.

These ox-peckers are much smaller birds than cattle egrets. They are about the same size as starlings, and closely related to them. Originally they probably fed, like cattle egrets, on insects disturbed by the movements of their partners, as well as on the ticks which grow in their skins. Today, however, they feed only on these ticks and on the various flies which settle on their partners' bodies.

They seldom descend to the ground and will generally fly into trees only when someone disturbs them. Otherwise they spend the whole of their lives on the backs of antelopes, domestic cattle, buffalo, zebra, wart-hogs and rhinoceroses, even conducting their courtship displays and mating there. When their hosts wade into water to drink, the ox-peckers remain on their backs, except in the case of the wart-hog. When this animal visits a water-hole it likes to wallow in the mud, so the attendant birds fly into a nearby tree until it has finished.

To enable these birds to run about all over the bodies of their hosts their toes are capable of gripping and are provided with sharp claws, like those of the woodpecker. The tail, too, is stiff like a woodpecker's, to give additional support when the bird clings to the flanks of its host.

Besides the help they give in removing ticks from the partners' skins, ox-peckers also act as sentinels to warn them of the approach of danger. And danger often means man. When he is first seen he may be several hundred yards away. The birds immediately begin to utter warning cries, which become louder and more insistent as he comes nearer. The hosts finally run off, with the birds still clinging to their backs. Ox-peckers are not popular with the big-game hunter, for too often they give warning to the animal he wants to shoot just as he is getting within range. So far as is known, such cries are given only if a man is approaching, and never when any other animal is sighted.

One curious fact about these warning cries is that they are always given by the birds when they are perched on any kind of wild animal, but never if they are on domestic animals. Then they will let anyone approach without showing fear or uttering cries. In these circumstances they can in fact become surprisingly tame and trusting. They seem to know that man is only a danger to wild animals, and will not harm domestic cattle.

The ox-pecker's most remarkable association is with the rhinoceros – it is in fact often called the rhinoceros bird. Between the two species there seems to be a particularly strong bond, and in parts of Africa it is rare to see a rhino without its accompanying birds. Even when one has been shot the birds will often refuse to leave the carcass unless they are actually chased away. The rhinoceros has very poor eyesight, so it probably benefits more than most other animals from the warnings of the ox-peckers. It is even said that for rhinos the birds give louder and more frequent warnings than they do for any other animal, as though they know about the rhino's poor eyesight.

There is a difference of opinion among experts as to whether ox-peckers can live without feeding on ticks. Many attempts have been made to keep them in captivity, experimenting with all kinds of foods, but nearly always they have died after a short time. It has been suggested that they cannot live for long without mammal blood that has been changed by being sucked into ticks' bodies. This may well be so, though at least one person claims to have kept the birds alive for a considerable time by feeding them on minced raw meat. Whatever the truth, it is at least certain that without their diet of ticks they do not easily survive.

Crabs, as we have seen in earlier chapters, enter into partnership with a number of different species of animals for mutual protection, but even they cannot rival the ants in the variety of their partnerships. Experts have calculated that in the nests of the twenty-seven different species of British ants more than one thousand different kinds of guests have been found. Many of these are parasites, preying upon their hosts and destroying their young, but many others enter into genuine partnerships with the ants, giving something in return for being allowed to enjoy the safety and shelter of the nest.

The best known of all the ant partners are the aphids: the greenfly and the blackfly. Certain kinds of ants keep aphids in herds and milk them in the same way as a dairy farmer looks after his cattle. In order to milk an aphid the ant stands behind it and strokes its body many times in quick succession with its antennae. In a short time a drop of clear liquid appears from the hind end of the aphid's body, and is soon lapped up by the ant.

Production of this clear sweet liquid, known as honey-dew, is a normal physiological process with all aphids. These tiny insects feed only on plant juices, having jaws which are adapted for piercing and sucking. Plant sap contains very large amounts of sugar and only small amounts of the other food materials that are equally necessary to an animal. In order to get enough of these the aphids have to gather a great deal of sap, and in doing so they take in much more sugar than they need. So their digestive system takes out all the necessary food materials and the surplus sugar is allowed to pass right through the body, to be discharged as honey-dew, the clear sweet liquid which the ants lap up.

Not all ants are interested in honey-dew. Some are flesh eaters, killing and eating other small animals, while others prefer seeds. Many kinds, though, seem to have a craving for sweet things, and it is these which love honey-dew. There are many different kinds of aphids, and each has its own particular food plant. The flavour of the honey-dew produced must vary accordingly, because it is only certain species of aphids which interest ants.

The small black lawn ant is one of the most skilful aphid farmers. It looks after and milks herds of aphids living on nearby plants. It often builds little mud sheds on stems and on leaf stalks, and in these the aphids can hide from their enemies. Sometimes the ants will carry some of their herd back to the nest at night, returning them to the plants in the morning. If the ants are not satisfied with the number of aphids on the plants near their nest they will fetch others from plants farther away in order to increase the size of their herds.

Aphids do not always live above ground. There are certain kinds which live underground, sucking juices from plant roots. Several kinds of ants farm these aphids, collecting them from farther afield and bringing them to the roots of plants which are growing above and around the nest. Underground aphids are milked in just the same way as those on leaves and stems.

In their dealings with aphids ants often show considerable foresight and intelligence. The common yellow ant of the fields farms two kinds of aphids, an underground kind which lives on grass roots running through the nest and an aerial variety which lives on plant stems and leaves. During the autumn the ants collect the tiny dark eggs of the second kind and carry them back to the nest for protection during the winter. With the arrival of spring they are taken out of the nest and placed on the correct food plants, where they will found a colony for the ants to milk throughout the summer.

American scientists, in studying the partnership between a certain ant and a type of aphid which lives on corn roots, have discovered an even more remarkable example of 'intelligent' behaviour in ants. The

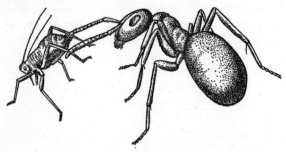

An ant milking an aphid

aphid eggs are collected and stored in the nest for the winter. When they hatch out in early spring the corn roots are not developed sufficiently to provide enough food for the young aphids. So when the ants carry the newly hatched aphids out of their nests they dig down into the ground and place them on the roots of other plants. A few weeks later, when the corn has started into vigorous growth, the aphids are collected from their temporary homes and transferred to the corn roots.

Closely related to the aphids, and also living on plant juices, are other tiny insects called mealy bugs and scale insects. These, too, are cultivated and milked by ants. One kind, the pineapple mealy bug of Hawaii, which causes great damage to pineapple plantations, has become so dependent upon ants that unless it is regularly milked it dies, suffocated by an accumulation of honey-dew and dust. If only the planter can rid his field of ants he has nothing to fear from the mealy bugs. On the other hand a field which is clear of mealy bugs can soon become heavily infested through the efforts of the ants, which will bring them from neighbouring fields and pasture them on the unoccupied pineapple plants.

Perhaps the most unusual ant guest is the caterpillar of the large blue butterfly, *Maculinea arion*. How the partnership between the caterpillar and the ants was discovered is an interesting story.

By the end of the nineteenth century the life histories of all our British butterflies, with the exception of the large blue, were known, and most of them had been bred in captivity. Every caterpillar undergoes four moults during its life, after which it changes into a chrysalis or pupa. No one, however, had ever found a large blue caterpillar between the third moult and chrysalis stages. It seemed that before the fourth moult the caterpillars vanished completely, and some time later the adult butterflies suddenly appeared – from where no one knew.

All attempts to rear them in captivity failed. Up to the third moult they thrived on a diet of wild thyme flowers, which are their natural food. But after this moult they invariably lost all interest in the flowers, and refused to eat everything else which was offered to them. At the same time it was noticed that they began wandering about the cage as though they were lost, and in a little while they would lie down and die.

The mystery was not finally solved until the summer of 1915 when F. W. Frohawk, a great authority on butterflies, was visiting Cornwall with another enthusiast, Dr Chapman. They were searching for caterpillars among wild thyme plants when Dr Chapman pulled one up which was growing on an ants' nest. And there, lying in a chamber of the nest which had been exposed, was a chrysalis. It was not, they knew, the chrysalis of any other British butterfly, so it must be that of the large blue. Unfortunately this one had been damaged by the thyme roots as they were torn out of the earth. But the two men dissected it, and found that its stomach was filled with ant grubs.

Much still remained to be found out before the complete story could be pieced together. Two other butterfly experts, Captain Purefoy and

Mr L. W. Newman, founder of the famous butterfly farm assisted in this
work. In order to find out exactly what happened in the ants' nest
Captain Purefoy made a miniature ant hill in a walnut shell, and Mr
Newman supplied him with large blue caterpillars.

As a result of their patient observations we now know the whole
story. After the third moult the caterpillar leaves the thyme plant on
which it has been feeding and wanders aimlessly about. Sooner or later
it will probably meet an ant, which immediately shows great interest in
it. At this stage it has developed a gland on its back and it is to this that
the ant goes. As it caresses the gland with its feelers drops of sweet
liquid are produced and eagerly lapped up, and this process continues
for some time. Then suddenly the caterpillar hunches itself up in such
a way that the ant can pick it up by the scruff of its neck and carry it
back to the nest.

Once inside it is treated like an honoured guest, the ants feeding it
with their own grubs. After some weeks, when it has grown to full size,
it ceases to feed and goes into hibernation for the winter. When spring
comes round it wakes up again, feeds for a while, and then changes at
last to a chrysalis. A few weeks later the adult butterfly emerges from
the chrysalis case, makes its way out of the nest, and climbs up the
nearest grass stalk. Here it spreads its wings, waits for them to dry and
harden in the sun, and then flies away.

All attempts to rear the caterpillars after the third moult on any food
other than ant grubs have failed. It seems therefore that the grubs must
contain some substance which is essential to the caterpillar's development. Certainly the butterfly seems to get most of the benefit from this
partnership, which is yet another example of the sacrifices which ants
are prepared to make in return for the coveted drops of sweet liquid.

Caterpillars of several other blue butterflies are often found with ant
attendants, though none of these enter into such an intimate relationship
with the ants as the large blue. All of them have a single gland opening
on the back of the tenth segment which produces drops of sweet liquid
when stimulated by the ants' antennae.

Although these other caterpillars are not taken into the shelter of the
nests, they do enjoy a considerable advantage from the almost constant
attention of the ants. Insect enemies will not attack them while the ants
are around.

Cynips kollari, 109
Cyprina, 30

Danaus plexippus, 162
Date mussel, 42
Deer, 13–17
Dendroaspis angusticeps, 126; *D. poly-lepis*, 126
Dendrobates, 158
Desmodus rotundus, 106
Devil's coach-horse, 157
Dicrostichus magnificus, 83
Diodon hystrix, 58
Diplopoda, 122
Diprion pini, 107; *D. sertifer*, 107
Diptera, 100, 106, 161
Dispholidus typus, 124
Dog whelk, 20–1, 32, 49–50
Dromia vulgaris, 145
Duiker, 26

Earwig, 157
Echinoderms, 62–5
Elapidae, 124–8
Elephant, 18
Encarsis formosa, 113
Ensis ensis, 30; *E. siliqua*, 30
Eriosoma lanigerum, 151
Eristalis vinetorum, 163
Eumenes coarctata, 114
Eupagurus bernhardus, 120

Fish:
    archer, 72–5; bat-, 85; clown, 120; cod, 119–20, 143; conger eel, 143; coral, 119–20; damsel, 119–20; deep-sea angler, 85; electric, 132–40; cat-fish, electric, 138, 140; eel, electric, 136–8, 140; Father lasher, 56–7; hag-, 67; herring, 45; jelly-, 62, 117, 119; knife-, 135–8, 140; lamprey, 67–70; long-spined sea scorpion, 56; mackerel, 59, 119; mormyroids, 135–8, 140; octopus, 66–7, 143; pearl-, 44; pike, 18; piranha, 18–20; plaice, 139, 141–2; porcupine globe, 58; porpoise, 70; puffer, 58; ray, 57, 139–40; salmon, 68, 139; saw-, 59–60; shark, 18–20, 59, 70; skate, 57, 139–40; spear-, 59; stargazer, 140; sting ray, 57–8; sword-, 59–60; torpedo ray, 139–40; tunny, 59; turbot, 141–2; weever (sea cat, sea dragon, sting bull, sting fish), 56; whiting, 119–20
Flea, 61, 102–3, 105
Fly:
    alder, 150; bee robber, 162; caddis, 37–8; drone, 161; hover-, 161, 163; ichneumon, 107–12, 115, 131; lan-tern, 152; sedge, 37; snake-, 93, 150

Frog, 75, 79, 87, 142, 157–8
Frogfish, 85
Frog-hopper, 104, 115, 150–1
Furrow shell, 32

Gaper, 30, 41
Gazelle, Mongolian, 26
Giraffe, 13, 16–17
Glowworm, 87
Goat, 13
Goat-antelope, 25
Grasshopper, 153, 167
Greenfly, 169
Gribble, 43
Gymnarchus niloticus, 133–5

Haemopis sanguisuga, 97
Hare, Scottish blue, 149
Hedgehog, 60–1
Heliconiidae, 160
Hemiptera, 104, 150
Hemiteles nannus, 110
Hiatella arctica, 42; *H. gallicana*, 42
Hippolyte varians, 141
Hippopotamus, 13, 166
Hirudinea, 96
Hirudo medicinalis, 97–8
Hornet, 108
Horse, 13, 21, 23, 25
Hydrophiidae, 126–8
Hymenoptera, 107–13, 157, 161
Hystrix cristata, 61

Ixodes ricinus, 98

Kangaroo, 21–2

Lace-wing, 93, 150
Lachesis muta, 127
Lac insect, 151
Ladybird, 115, 131, 157
Lanice conchilega, 36
Leaf-hopper, 104
Leech, 96–8, 165–6
Lice, 102–5
Limenitis archippus, 162
Limpet, 20, 48, 50
Litomastix, 112
Lizard, 87, 99, 156–7
Lizard tick, 99
Lithophagus lithophagus, 42
Lobster, 44, 66–7, 122, 146
Lophius americanus, 85; *L. piscatorius*, 84–6
Lucanus, cervus, 157

Macroclemmys temmincki, 86
Maculinea arion, 171
Malapterurus electricus, 138
Mallophaga, 102
Mallophora bomboides, 162